EVERYDAY LIFE IN
ANGLO-SAXON TIMES

The EVERYDAY LIFE series is one of the
best known and most respected of all historical
works, giving detailed insight into the
background life of a particular period.
This edition provides an invaluable and
vivid picture of everyday life in Anglo-
Saxon times from their invasion of Roman
Britain to the coming of the Normans.

The *New Statesman* has commended the
Quennells' 'rare gift for arousing historical
imagination', and this volume is an
outstanding account of how ordinary
people lived during the great changes in
everyday life caused by the Anglo-Saxon
invasions.

3cde

Other EVERYDAY LIFE books

published by Carousel Books

MARJORIE and C. H. B. QUENNELL

EVERYDAY LIFE IN
ANGLO-SAXON TIMES

Carousel Editor: Anne Wood

CAROUSEL BOOKS
A DIVISION OF TRANSWORLD PUBLISHERS LTD
A NATIONAL GENERAL COMPANY

EVERYDAY LIFE IN ANGLO-SAXON TIMES

A CAROUSEL BOOK 0 552 54016 1

Originally published in Great Britain
by B. T. Batsford Ltd. as *Everyday Life in Anglo-Saxon, Viking and Norman Times*

PRINTING HISTORY
Batsford edition published 1924
Batsford revised edition (*Everyday Life in Roman and Anglo-Saxon Times*)
published 1959
Batsford 5th impression published 1969
Carousel edition published 1972

Carousel Books are published by Transworld Publishers Ltd.,
Cavendish House, 57–59 Uxbridge Road,
Ealing, London, W.5

Made and printed in Great Britain by
Cox & Wyman Ltd., London, Reading and Fakenham

PREFACE

THE boys and girls for whom we write, may have read the
Life of Agricola, by Tacitus, and so know the fine Epilogue with
which it closes.

'And I would lay this charge on his daughter and his wife – so
to reverence the memory of their father, and husband, that they
revolve within them all that he said and did, and to cherish the
form and the fashion of his soul, rather than of his body; it is not
that I would forbid the making of statues, shaped in marble or
bronze, but that as the human face, so is its copy – futile and
perishing, while the form of the mind is eternal, to be expressed,
not through the alien medium of art and its material, but sever-
ally by each man in the fashion of his own life.'

Tacitus was writing of the character of his father-in-law,
Agricola, and gave us at the same time a hint of what we should
look for in history. If only the spirit is eternal, it is very obvious
that we must make diligent search for the principles which have
animated men in the past and helped them to fashion their
souls. To search for motive is apt to be an arid study; political
history, and its recital of how statesmen have bested their friends,
and ruined their enemies, makes dull reading, unless it is inspired.
There remains the possibility of judging men by their works. This
was the only method in the Prehistoric periods, and it is on
the whole a very safe one.
– In the wide region of Statecraft, we can watch the efforts of
man to govern himself. The hill forts could only have been formed
under some system of tribal government, and in the historic
period, we find Kings and Empires, Tyrannies, Democracies, and
Republics, tried one after the other, in man's search for the proper
method of living.

From the time of the Roman Occupation, so far as Europe was
concerned, Christianity was destined to become the great force

by which men set the 'fashion of their souls'; it civilized men again after the dark ages following on the fall of Rome, and inspired the Crusades. Churches were planned to be cruciform, and the figure of Christ was cut in stone, and glowed in the jewelled glass of a thousand windows.

It follows, then, that we are in sympathy with all the people, who, since A.D. was used in the calender, have been confronted with similar problems of life and death, of joy and sorrow, and of how life is to be made sweet and wholesome.

The statesman reads history to find how man can be helped to this end, and his trouble is the same as ours, how to make the dry bones live. There are times of enlightenment.

Our readers will sometimes have seen visions, and dreamed dreams. There are days, or better still nights, when the tired body is sloughed off, and the brain rides untrammelled, and we understand the meaning of things. The time curtains roll back a little on one side, and we have a walking part in the scene; we may not speak to the principal actors, but we are close to them; we catch the fragrance of Wolsey's orange as he passes along, and the figures of history become instead of names, men and women of flesh and blood.

We begin to form certain opinions of our own; one period may seem brave and cheerful, another dark and gloomy. For this reason, perhaps, history has been very much concerned with the doings of great men; even the terrible villains serve the useful purpose of shadow in the picture, and throw into relief the brightness of the heroes. If these have been rather dispensers of Death, than saviours of life, like Pasteur, then it is our own fault for having worshipped at the wrong shrine. This question of the atmosphere of history is worth testing by our own experience; this may be limited, but we can try to find out why a particular school, or form, or term, or individual, will leave an impression on our minds. The importance of history, or tradition, is that it gives us a standard against which we can measure our own effort, and as history is concerned just as much with work as war, so work is concerned with the doings of untold myriads of individuals much the same as ourselves.

MARJORIE AND C. H. B. QUENNELL

CONTENTS

ACKNOWLEDGMENT

The Authors and Publishers wish to thank the following for permission to reproduce these illustrations:

Fig. 6 from *Medieval Archaeology* (Journal of the Society for Medieval Archaeology), Volume I, 1957; and Fig. 17 from *Late Saxon and Viking Art* by T. D. Kendrick (Methuen & Co. Ltd.)

LIST OF ILLUSTRATIONS

BIBLIOGRAPHY

Hunter Blair, P., *Anglo-Saxon England* (Cambridge, 1956).

Bone, Gavin, *Anglo-Saxon Poetry* (Oxford, 1944).

Baldwin Brown, G., *The Arts in Early England*. Six volumes (John Murray, 1925).

Chadwick, H. M., *The Heroic Age* (Cambridge, 1912).

Chadwick, H. M. and N. K., *The Growth of Literature* (Cambridge, 1932).

Clapham, A. W., *English Romanesque Architecture before the Conquest* (Oxford, 1930).

Collingwood, R. G. and Myers, J. N. L., *Roman Britain and the English Settlements* (Oxford, 1945).

Dasent, G. W., *The Story of Burnt Njal* (Dent, Everyman Library), N. D.

Duckett, Eleanor, *Anglo-Saxon Saints and Scholars* (Macmillan, 1947).

Clark Hall, J. R., *Beowulf* (Cambridge, 1914).

Hight, G. A., *The Saga of Grettir the Strong* (Dent, Everyman Library, 1929).

Hodgkin, R. H., *History of the Anglo-Saxons* (Cambridge, 1935).

Jessup, Ronald, *Anglo-Saxon Jewellery* (Faber, 1950).

Kendrick, T. D., *Anglo-Saxon Art* (Methuen, 1938).

Kendrick, T. D., *A History of the Vikings* (Methuen, 1930).

Kendrick, T. D., *Late Saxon and Viking Art* (Methuen, 1949).

Leeds, E. T., *Early Anglo-Saxon Art and Archaeology* (Oxford, 1936).

Monsen, Erling, *Heimskringla, or the lives of the Norse Kings* (Heffer, 1931).

Page, R. I., *Life in Anglo-Saxon England* (Batsford, 1970).

Pochin Mould, D. D. C., *Scotland of the Saints* (Batsford, 1952).

Pochin Mould, D. D. C., *Ireland of the Saints* (Batsford, 1953).

Stenton, F. M., *Anglo-Saxon England* (Oxford, 1943).

Sutton Hoo Ship Burial (British Museum, 1947).

Talbot Rice, D., *English Art, 871–1110* (Oxford, 1952).

Thompson, A. H., *Bede* (Oxford, 1935).

Wilson, D. M., *The Anglo-Saxons* (Thames and Hudson, 1960).

THE COMING OF THE ENGLISH

THE collapse of Roman rule in Britain was a gradual process and the incursions of those people we know as Anglo-Saxons took place over a long period of time. The Roman army and the Roman civil service officially withdrew from Britain about the year 410, but traces of Roman government and administration survived for many years after this: gradually, however, Roman civilization was forgotten, the towns were abandoned and the straight Roman roads fell into decay. At Silchester an intruder penetrated one of the many deserted houses of the Roman town and camped there for a short time, lighting a fire in the middle of the mosaic floor. Neglect was the chief cause of the downfall of Roman institutions in England.

The people who came to settle in England at the end of the Roman period came from Holland, North Germany, and Denmark. The Venerable Bede, an Anglo-Saxon monk of the joint monastery of Monkwearmouth and Jarrow, writing nearly two hundred years after the event, in about 730, said, 'They came from three very powerful nations of Germany, namely the Saxons, Angles, and Jutes. From the Jutes are descended the people of Kent and the Isle of Wight and also those in the province of the West Saxons, who are to this day called the Jutes, situated opposite the Isle of Wight. From the Saxons are descended the

East Saxons, the South Saxons, and the West Saxons. From the Angles are descended the East Angles, the Middle Angles, the Mercians, and all the race of the Northumbrians.' For convenience these various peoples are known as the Anglo-Saxons or, more simply, the Saxons. The Anglo-Saxons started to call themselves Engle and it is from this word that the name 'English' is derived; the term England was not however used until the eleventh century. The Saxon name survives in the names of the counties of Essex and Sussex, while the Eastern counties of Norfolk, Suffolk, and Cambridgeshire are still referred to by their ancient name – East Anglia.

The first Anglo-Saxons came to England before the end of the Roman period as professional soldiers who helped to defend the country against threatening invaders from Holland, Ireland, and Scotland. They garrisoned the forts of the Saxon shore, which are spread along the Eastern coast of England from Hampshire to Norfolk, and presumably helped to fortify the new fortresses (like that at Caernarvon) on the Welsh coast. They presumably settled down with their families in the rich countryside of Roman Britain and, when the Romans withdrew from Britain they refused to be interested in the defence of the foreign country in which they had settled and probably welcomed the incursions of their cousins from across the North Sea who, as a result of the general land hunger of the period wanted to find a place in which they could settle in peace. The Anglo-Saxons came in small bands – perhaps such a band was that led by Hengest to the Isle of Thanet in 449 – but gradually these bands built themselves up into a mighty military force which was ultimately to conquer Britain.

Dimly across the centuries we hear faint echoes of

the resistance that met the Saxons. From the conflicting accounts of coloured legend and dry history we know of a leader named Arthur who, in the last half of the fifth century, fought twelve battles against the Anglo-Saxons and won all of them. He seems to have organized a highly mobile army of Romanized Britons, which went to the aid of the petty kings and chieftains who were struggling against the overwhelming forces of the Anglo-Saxons. The Anglo-Saxon conquest of England was not finally completed, however, until Egbert, King of Wessex, won the last battle against the Britons in 815.

The conquered Britons gradually became submerged in the Saxon population, or else fled to those parts of the British Isles – Scotland, Wales, and Ireland – where the Britons were strong enough to retain political power. It was in these outlying countries that Christianity, introduced into the British Isles by the Romans, survived. Little else remained to remind the Briton or the Saxon of the once powerful Roman Empire. In England many of the great Roman buildings fell into decay; their meaning was lost and they became mysteries, referred to with awe as the works of giants.

Not all the buildings fell into disuse. Many of the towns survived, although not in the splendour of their Roman heyday. London is described by Bede as 'the metropolis of the East Saxons . . ., a market place of many people coming by land and sea'. But the elaborate machinery of Roman town government was lost and the towns were only inhabited by a few merchants and craftsmen. Some towns, Silchester and Wroxeter, for example, disappeared completely, but the Roman fountains were still playing at Carlisle when St. Cuthbert visited it, towards the end of the seventh century. The Kentish kings at the end of the sixth century had established their court within the ruins of the Roman city of Canterbury, where some hundred years previously a few Saxon families had built some rather squalid huts in an open space not far from the great Roman theatre. With the coming of Christianity the missionaries used the ancient cities as the centres of their bishoprics, ultimately establishing their cathedrals there. Later on some of the larger cities, like St. Albans, became the seats of large monasteries and the monks used the tumbledown Roman buildings as a quarry for building their churches and living quarters. The walls of many of the Roman cities stood until the Middle Ages when, as at Chester, Lincoln, and Colchester, the Roman walls were incorporated into the city walls. The Roman villa system, however, disappeared completely and the continental invaders laid the foundations of many of the English villages which exist today.

What caused the Anglo-Saxon invasions? Like so many invasions of history and prehistory the roots are hidden deep.

The Anglo-Saxons came to England as a result of disturbance in Central Asia. The Huns came from there, and attacked their neighbours, the Goths, who moved across the Danube, and the Rhine, into the Roman Empire. The Goths captured Rome, and sacked it in 410, and the movement was not stopped until Attila, the King of the Huns, was defeated at Châlons in 451. Another Teutonic people, the Franks, moved into France for the same reason and reached the Loire by 489.

'Westward Ho!' is a very old cry, but in the days of which we are writing it was one fraught with awful peril for civilization. The Roman Empire spelled

civilization, and it was a wonderful fabric. The
Empire was bounded by the Danube and the Rhine,
and across these rivers surged hordes of pagan barbarians, as in older days still the Achaeans had borne
down on the Mycenaeans in Greece.

Very truly the historians talk of the Dark Ages; yet
through the Darkness comes flashes. If we know little
of the period, yet what is known is always coloured by
life and movement. On one page we shall have to write
of Vikings, of bloodshed and battles under the standard
of the Raven; on another, of the saving of souls by men
like Columba, Augustine, Paulinus, and Aidan. Here
in England Christianity had become the great central
fact of man's existence, and it was assailed by Odin,
and Thor the god of Thunder. It will be part of our
tale to show how the Christian Church saved Western
civilization. It was a long fight, and before the battle
was won Christianity was assailed from another
quarter.

Mohammed was born about 570, and his followers
conquered Egypt and Palestine 634–40, and Persia in
651. By 709 they had taken North Africa from the
Byzantine Empire, and Spain in 711 from the Visi-
goths. Their further inroads were not stopped until
they were defeated by Charles Martel near Poitiers in
732. This was only the beginning of the long struggle
between the Cross and Crescent, which was to cul-
minate later in the Crusades. Enough has been written
to show that when the Anglo-Saxons came to England,
they were not moved to do so because they felt in need
of a holiday, but were forced to it by the stress of cir-
cumstance. One point should be noted. In their early
migrations they had come into contact with Gothic
culture in South Russia, and their love of colour and
jewellery can probably be traced back to this source.

The Anglo-Saxon Chronicle, compiled in the time of Alfred, 891–2, should be consulted for the details of the invasion. As we do not wish to stain these pages too deeply in blood, we shall content ourselves with one quotation from Bede, to show how desperate the struggle was.

Public as well as private structures were over-turned; the priests were everywhere slain before the altars; the prelates and the people, without any respect of persons, were destroyed with fire and sword; nor was there any to bury those who had been thus cruelly slaughtered. Some of the miserable remainder being taken in the mountains, were butchered in heaps. Others, spent with hunger, came forth and submitted themselves to the enemy for food, being destined to undergo perpetual ser-vitude if they were not killed on the spot.

This passage gives a far better idea than any words of ours of what the impact of barbarism meant to the Romano-British civilization, and we are apt to forget the debt we may owe to the Britons today, in keeping Christianity alive in the West. In fact, we may not even think of them as Christians, until we remember that St. Alban was martyred as early as 304, here in England. St Patrick went to Ireland about 432 and it was the Irish Church which sent Colomba to Iona about 563, and from Iona, Aidan went at a later date to Holy Isle, as we shall presently see. We must always remember that Great Britain was an outlier on the Roman Empire; a North-West Province which was the outpost of its civilization, and by its island position cut off from Rome by the barbarian inroads. It may well be that the whole history of this country would have been different, if the Irish Church had not humanized life in the West, while the Anglo-Saxons were giving a very fair imitation of the Devil and all his works elsewhere.

Before we trace the work of the Church in more detail, it may be well to go back and endeavour to find out if our Anglo-Saxon ancestors had any other qualities wherewith to qualify their ferocity.

Tacitus, who knew the breed, wrote. 'They live apart, each by himself, as woodside, plain, or fresh spring attracts him' and this has remained a characteristic of Englishmen ever since; they have little civic pride, but love the country. Tacitus of course did not mean solitary men living by themselves, or even single families, as today, in modest little houses in the suburbs. Even as late as the time of Sir Thomas More, we read that he built himself a house at Chelsea, where he lived with his wife, his son, and his daughter-in-law, his three daughters, and their husbands, with eleven grandchildren. In Anglo-Saxon times the families which lived together were even larger than this, and more like a tribe or clan. Bede always counts, not the number of inhabitants in a province, but tells you how many families it contained. He also throws an interesting sidelight on family customs. He wrote of one 'Orric, surnamed Oisc, from whom the kings of Kent are wont to be called Oiscings', and again 'The son of Tytilus whose father was Uuffa, from whom the kings of the East Angles are called Uuffings.' If we turn again to Bede we find that the kings at first were what we should call chiefs, 'for those Ancient Saxons have no king, but several lords that rule their nation; and on whomsoever the lot falls, him they follow and obey during the war; but as soon as the war is ended, all those lords are again equal in power'. When the

Saxons came to England, we must think of these chiefs settling down, and calling their home Uuffingham, because it was the home of the Uuffings, who were the descendants of Uuffa.

From such simple beginnings our English villages have grown up. The chief built his Hall, and grouped around it were the huts of his followers, and the bowers for the women-folk. The village had a meeting-place, or moot, where important decisions were taken; it also had a well or a spring for water. The whole was girt round with a ditch and bank, with a palisaded fence on top. There were the common fields, and outside all the mark, where the stranger coming must blow his horn or risk death. The freeman was the freeholder of part of the land, and there cannot have been many slaves in the bands of warriors who came first, but later the Britons who were captured were enslaved, and as society became more settled, and the chieftains became kings, some men went up, and others sank into a servile class.

Domesday Book, completed in 1086, mentions parishes of the time of Edward the Confessor which still remain, and which had their beginnings in the time we write of. The hall of the chief became the hall of the lord, and his chapel, built when he became a Christian, developed into the parish church. Bede writes of an inn, and there would have been a mill for grinding corn – a water mill, for instance, has recently been discovered and excavated at Old Windsor, Berkshire.

This is the outline on to which we have to graft fuller details, and our first step will be to familiarize ourselves with the appearance of the Anglo-Saxons, so that we may be able to fit them into the picture.

We may take it that the dress of the first Saxons who

arrived here resembled that illustrated in *Prehistoric Times*; this again was like that of the barbarians, and must have been common to the tribes outside the Empire, across the Rhine and Danube. The Anglo-Saxon dress was a development of this.

A Thane wore a shirt, and breeches, sometimes to the ankles, and at others cut off at the knee, when hose like leggings were added, and fastened by cross garters

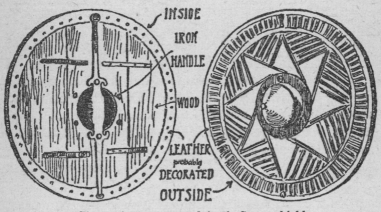

INSIDE
IRON
HANDLE
WOOD
LEATHER
probably
DECORATED
OUTSIDE

Fig. 1 A reconstructed Anglo-Saxon shield

which were part of the leather shoes. These latter were sometimes gilded. The breeches were probably fastened at the waist, by a belt passed through loops. Over the shirt, a wool, or linen, tunic reaching to the knee was worn. This was belted at the waist, and had long sleeves tight at the wrist, and fastened with metal clasps. The cloak was fastened on breast or shoulder with a brooch. For everyday use caps of Phrygian shape were worn.

A chieftain of some importance wore a tunic which was a coat of mail formed of iron rings sewn on to the strong cloth. His helmet had an iron frame, filled in

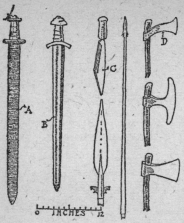

Fig. 2 Saxon and Viking arms

between with horn with a boar on the crest (see Beowulf, page 30). The spear was the commonest weapon in the early pagan days; sometimes it had wings on it (fig. 2) and the socket was formed by hammering the iron round until the sides met. The shaft of ash, 6 to 7 feet long, had an iron ferrule. Some were thrown as javelins. The early swords were formidable weapons, a yard long, with a wooden scabbard (fig. 2, A). The later types had a tapered blade, as (fig. 2, B); Scramas-axes were sword-like knives, as (fig. 2, C).

Battle-axes were used, and some were thrown (fig. 2, D). Shields were of wood, sometimes covered with hide, painted or set with semi-precious stones or gilt-bronze mounts, sometimes oval, and at others round. They measured between 1 foot 6 inches and 3 feet in diameter. Fig. 1 shows the hand-grip of one. The bow was not very much used.

Women were dressed in one linen undergarment, and a tunic to the feet. Sometimes there were two tunics girdled at the waist, the inner having long sleeves, and the outer shorter and wider ones. Over these came the mantle, hanging down at back and front, in a way which suggests a poncho pattern with central hole for the head. The brooches, which we discuss later, appear to have been worn in pairs. The head was covered with a silk or linen wrap. The women wore girdles (girdle hangers like chatelaines

have been found in their graves), and they had little
bags.

They adorned themselves with fine barbaric neck-
laces; big lumps of amber, crystal, amethyst, or beads
of glass coloured in many ways. One in the British
Museum has barrel-shaped gold beads which alternate
with gold-mounted garnet pendants. Sometimes these
were worn festooned across the chest, or as bracelets.

We cannot illustrate all the beautiful things which
were used. Belts had jewelled buckles, and there were
armlets, and rings. Pins of all patterns were made;
Ireland was the home of what are called hand-pins,
with the head cranked like a modern tie-pin. The
horse was trapped out as beautifully as his master.
Children's dress was a miniature edition of that of
their parents.

The ceorl would have worn the same type of
clothes as his master, but everything would have been
simpler and rougher. He carried no sword. This was
the weapon of the earl or thane.

This will be a good place in which to show the
development of the brooches which were used to
fasten the cloaks. These can be traced back to South
Russia, where they were used by the Goths. Fig. 3 has
been drawn to show some of the developments of the
main types of brooch. Fig. 3, probably East Anglian, is
perhaps as early as the fifth century, and the same
pattern, with the horse-like head on the foot, is found
as well in Scandinavia. All these brooches are glorified
versions of our old friend the safety-pin, but with a
spring on both sides of the head (see *Prehistoric Times*,
which shows the beginnings in the Bronze and Early
Iron Ages).

Fig. 3, 2, shows the next development. The knobs

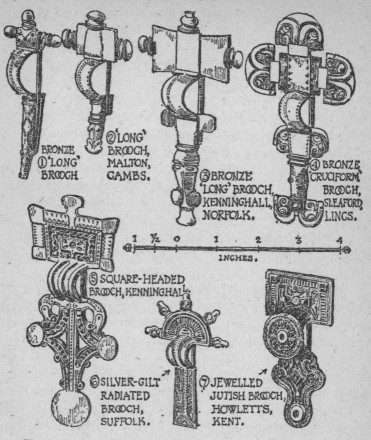

Fig. 3 Early (Pagan) Anglo-Saxon brooches (*British Museum*)

on the bar are now cast in one piece with the brooch. This type dates from the end of the fifth century. Fig. 3, 3 shows a further and later development. Fig. 3, 4, illustrates why this type is called 'cruciform'; it dates from the seventh century, and is a beautiful piece, with small silver panels on the arms of the cross, and garnet inlay on the nostrils of the horse. Fig. 3, 5 is a square-headed brooch which resembles types started in Den-

mark; this is earlier than Fig. 3, 4, dating from about
500. Fig. 3, 6 is a radiated brooch, of which parallels
have been found in the Crimea; this is a fifth-century
type. Fig. 3, 7 has its own peculiar Jutish design.

The Anglo-Saxons used as well circular brooches.
Sometimes they were plain and sometimes saucer-
shaped with a cast design in the centre. Occasionally
they were made of an embossed plate cemented on to a
disc with vertical edge, the pin at the back being
hinged.

The jewelled circular brooches found in Kent are
extraordinarily fine. Some are like the disc applied to
the bow of Fig. 3, 7. This is called the keystone brooch,
because the garnet inlays are mounted in the form of
wedges, like the keystones of an arch, the central boss
being of ivory, or some similar white substance. Others
are far more elaborately decorated with garnets and
blue glass to imitate lapis lazuli, and gold filigree
work applied to the background. The Kentish jewellery has parallels in the Rhineland and Italy, and its
best period is about the year 600.

There are quoit brooches, so called because of their
shape, made of silver, partly gilt. There were wonderful developments of the Early Iron Age penannular
types, shaped like an incomplete ring; some tenth-
century brooches had pins as much as two feet long.

Fine jewellery needs good material to show it off,
and there is evidence that the Anglo-Saxon women
were expert weavers. When William the Conqueror
returned from England to France for the first time,
his Norman subjects were astonished by the garments
he had obtained in England – they were much finer
than any that had ever been seen in France. Gold
threads have been found in graves, generally in a
position which suggests that they were originally

woven into a head-dress. This may have been produced in the same way as the ephod made for Aaron, 'they did beat the gold into thin plates, and cut it into wires, to work it in the blue, and in the purple, and in the scarlet, and in the fine linen, with cunning work'.

This joyous use of colour was not confined to costume, but was common to everything. King Alfred, for example, made his grandson Athelstan 'a knight unusually early, giving him a scarlet coat, a belt studded with diamonds and a Saxon sword with a golden scabbard'. He must have presented a very colourful appearance.

The materials of which we have been writing were of course woven on a loom, and drawings in the manuscripts suggest that this had been developed. As we last saw it (in *Prehistoric Times*) the warp was stretched by warp weights; now a bottom roller was added, which got rid of the weights; and enabled a greater length of material to be made. Blunt iron blades, like short two-edged swords, have been found in women's graves, and these are thought to have been used to pack the weft threads together on to those of the warp. The weaving was done as described in *Everyday Life in Prehistoric Times*.

An interesting object is the work-box (Fig. 4) which was found in a grave, and is now in the British Museum. It is of gilt-bronze and contained thread, wool, linen, and needles.

Here we may give a note on ecclesiastical costumes. In the priest's vestments the long white tunic became the alb. The upper tunic with looser and shorter sleeves, the dalmatic. The mantle developed into the chasuble, and its hood became the cope. The more important vestments were richly embroidered with gold and coloured thread.

There is also the traditional costume in which Our Lord and the Saints and Angels are always shown. First comes a long sleeved tunic, then there is a mantle, one end of which hangs down from the left shoulder in

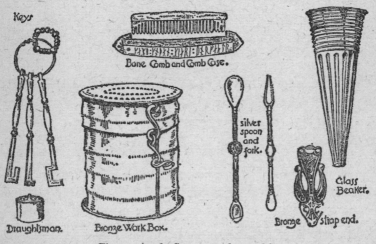

Keys

Bone Comb and Comb Case.

silver spoon and fork.

Glass Beaker.

Draughtsman.   Bronze Work Box.   Bronze Strap end.

Fig. 4 Anglo-Saxon workmanship

front, the remainder being taken behind the back, and passed under the right shoulder and across the front to be draped over the left arm or shoulder. This dress is much in the classical fashion of the Roman toga.

Having obtained some idea of the appearance of the Saxons, we must search for the local colour of their background, and we cannot do better than study Bede's History. Its date, about 730, makes it very important. The final conquest of the Britons, in 815, was approaching; the Danes had not yet appeared to plunder and destroy, so the picture given by Bede is of the apex of Anglo-Saxon civilization.

He opens with a description,

> Britain, an island in the ocean, formerly called Albion . . . excels for grain and trees, and is well adapted for feeding cattle and beasts of burden. It also produces vines in some places, and has plenty of land and water-fowls of several sorts; it is re-markable also for rivers abounding in fish, and plentiful springs. It has the greatest plenty of salmon and eels; seals are frequently taken, and dolphins, as also whales; besides many sorts of shell-fish, such as mussels, in which are often found excellent pearls of all colours, red, purple, violet, and green, but mostly white. There is also a great abundance of cockles, of which the scarlet dye is made; a most beautiful colour which never fades with the heat of the sun or the washing of the rain; but the older it is the more beautiful it becomes. It has both salt and hot springs, and from them flow rivers which furnish hot baths proper for all ages and sexes, and arranged according.

Bede mentions copper, iron, lead, silver, and jet,

> which is black and sparkling, glittering at the fire, and when heated drives away serpents; being warmed with rubbing, it holds fast whatever is applied to it, like amber. (He goes on to say) this island at present, contains five nations, the English, Britons, Scots (meaning the Irish), Picts, and Latins (Romanized Britons), each in its own peculiar dia-lect cultivating the sublime study of Divine truth. The Latin tongue is, by the study of the Scriptures, become common to all the rest.

Even in Bede's time, the people do not appear to have been town dwellers, because he writes,

The Island was *formerly* embellished with twenty-eight noble cities, besides innumerable castles, which were all strongly secured with walls, towers, gates, and locks. [Some of the Roman towns, though, were being used, because we read in 604] The East Saxons, who are divided from Kent by the river Thames, and border on the Eastern sea. Their metropolis is the city of London, which is situated on the bank of the aforesaid river, and is the mart of many nations resorting to it by sea and land.

We do not know how far the Roman Londinium had been destroyed, but there must have been considerable remains to influence the Saxon builders. Perhaps they patched them up here and there, and added timber buildings when new ones were necessary. Benedict Biscop, who built the monastery at Jarrow, where Bede lived, is said to have been 'the first person who introduced in England constructors of stone edifices, as well as the makers of glass windows', meaning of course the first after the Romans.

In 710, the king of the Picts wrote to Abbot Ceolfrid, of Jarrow, to send him architects 'to build a church in his nation after the Roman manner'. Mellitus, bishop of the East Saxons, built the church of St. Paul in the city of London, and this may have been in the Roman manner. We discuss this again in King Alfred's time.

We will now consider the hall of the Chief. This was to remain, until the days of Elizabeth, as the central feature of the house in which all the household met for meals and jollity. Even today, the big house in a village is very often called the Hall. The bowers, and kitchens, which at first were separate buildings, were gradually tacked on the body of the hall, until in the fourteenth and fifteenth centuries they all come under the same roof, and the modern house takes shape.

If we turn to Beowulf, the great Anglo-Saxon poem, we find the early type of hall described, and there are many interesting details of everyday life.

The only manuscript of Beowulf is in the British Museum. This dates from about 1000, but deals with life in the first half of the sixth century. The poem opens with an account of the passing of Scyld, the Warrior King, who lived in earlier days and gave the Danes their name of Scyldings. Scyld was carried down to his ship, and placed by the mast, the dead eyes looking ahead. Weapons and treasure were put aboard and, with his standard high above his head, the ship was pushed out on the flood, to sail into the unknown seas beyond the horizon. Then we read of Beowulf, who was a prince of the Geats, of the Baltic island of Gotland. He went to Denmark to visit Hrothgar, who had built a Mead Hall, named Heorot, as a habitation for his retainers. This hall was a lofty and gabled building of wood, and gold-bespangled, and the door was strengthened by forged bands. A pathed way led up to it. These were not sufficient to keep out the fiend Grendel, who came at night and carried off the warriors sleeping after the banquet. Men sought beds among the outbuildings to escape.

Then came Beowulf in his fresh tarred ship, over the sea. With him were fourteen champions, above whose cheek-guards shone the boar-images covered with gold. Their corslets were hard, hand-locked, and glistened, each gleaming ring of iron chinked in their harness. Landing in Denmark, they went to Heorot. Here they put their shields against the wall, and sat on the benches.

Hrothgar was not in the hall. He had a chamber close by where he sat with his nobles. Beowulf went there, by a path between, and explained his mission, and was after entertained at a banquet in the hall. Wealhtheow, the queen, entered and bore the mead cup to Beowulf. He and his men slept in the hall, and there came Grendel, and killed one man. The monster was attacked by Beowulf, but escaped, with the loss of an arm, only to die later in the mere where he lived.

Again there was a banquet, and the hall was decorated with gold embroidered tapestries. The song was sung, the gleeman's lay. Then mirth rose high, the noise of revelry was clearly heard; cup-bearers proffered wine from curious vessels. The men then slept in the hall.

They cleared the bench-boards, it was spread about with beds and bolsters. They set war-bucklers at their heads, the shining shield-wood. There on the bench, above each noble, was exposed the helmet, prominent in war, the ringed mail-coat, the proud spear-shaft. It was ever their practice to be ready for the fray at home or in the field.

But Grendel's mother came to avenge his death, and carried off a noble. Beowulf was not in the hall, having had a separate lodging assigned to him as a special honour. He went to the King's bower, and then led a band on horseback, who traced the steps of the monster to the mere. Here Beowulf put on his armour and went down into the lake, and swimming to the bottom, found there a cavern where no water harmed him in any way. Here was fought the fight with the she-wolf of the deep. His own sword failed him, but in the cavern he found an old titanic sword, and with it gained the victory, and having killed the mother, cut the head off the dead body of Grendel.

The watchers on the bank viewed the blood-stained waters with gloomy foreboding, and the disheartened Danes went home. Later Beowulf swam up with Grendel's head and found his own men waiting. They returned to Heorot, where once again there was great rejoicing, and Hrothgar made a fine speech congratulating Beowulf, but warned him that though God deals out to mankind many gifts, the soul's guardian may sleep, and man wax insolent and arrogant, and so be 'struck at the heart under his armour, by the piercing arrow – the crooked strange behests of the malignant spirit'.

Beowulf returned to the land of the Geats, and told his king, Hygelac, of his adventures, seated opposite him in the hall. Later he became king himself, and ruled well until his own land was oppressed by a dragon, 50 feet long, winged, and vomiting fire. The monster lived in a barrow, 'the primeval earth-dwelling contained within it rocky arches', and guarded there a hoard of treasure. A drinking bowl was stolen by a thrall, and the dragon ravaged the countryside in revenge. Then Beowulf, now an old man, girded on his armour for his last fight and, killing the dragon, was himself killed by it.

His funeral pyre was made on the cliff by the sea, and around it were hung helmets, shields, and corslets, and then Beowulf was laid in its midst. When his body was consumed by fire, they heaped up a barrow on the remains, and in it placed the treasure of the dragon, 'where it still exists, as unprofitable to men as it had been before'.

The poem is of extraordinary interest, because it gives the outlook on life of the ordinary man. With Bede we see the world through a monk's eyes, but in Beowulf we have the thoughts of the warrior. It must have been sung by poets in a thousand halls until some Saxon Homer set it out in proper form.

There are many details in the poem which suggest the hall of Heorot was a timber-framed building, rather like a glorified barn. We have attempted a reconstruction of the exterior in Fig. 5, and of the interior on the jacket.

Fig. 5   An imaginary reconstruction of an Anglo-Saxon homestead

One important detail of these early halls should be noted: the principal seat instead of being on a raised dais at the end, as it was in the later mediaeval halls, was placed in the centre of the north side. The chief guest had his seat opposite on the south side, and here was a window. Women sat on cross benches at the end. The fire was placed centrally.

Bede recounts how a traveller came to a village and entered a house where the neighbours were feasting. 'They sat long at supper and drank hard, with a great fire in the middle of the room; it happened that the sparks flew up and caught the top of the house, which being made of wattles and thatch, was presently in a flame.'

We see in Beowulf how there were sleeping-rooms in other buildings. In one saga we find that these were on the first floor, reached by an outer staircase, because a guest, going up to bed, opened the wrong door and fell into the mead vat under instead.

At Yeavering, Northumberland, traces of a hall similar to Heorot have been uncovered, by careful excavation, within the last few years. Traces of four halls of different periods were found, each nearly a hundred feet long. Two had porches at either end while the other two were rectangular in plan, but elaborately buttressed. Yeavering was a royal site and as a consequence there were a number of small halls surrounding the main hall. Most of these must be considered as the private halls of noble retainers; one was a servants' dormitory and one a pagan temple which was later put to Christian use. Unfortunately only the ground-plan of the houses survives, so it is practically impossible to reconstruct the upper works.

We know remarkably little about the physical construction of the Anglo-Saxon house used by the peasant and small farmer. Only the richer houses are described in the literature and, with the exception of a few weaving-sheds at Sutton Courtenay, Berkshire, and a few rather shapeless wooden houses excavated at

Bourton-on-the-Water, Gloucestershire, English arch-aeologists have not yet uncovered the remains of the houses of the farmer and the peasant. The English archaeologist must look to Germany and Scandinavia where a great deal of excavation and research has enabled us to build up a general picture of the poorer house of the period. It seems reasonable to assume that the Anglo-Saxons built houses in the manner of their Germanic forebears, houses of the type described by Tacitus.

Tacitus, writing in the first century A.D., said that

none of the Germanic peoples dwell in cities, and they do not even tolerate houses which are built in rows. They dwell apart, and at a distance from one another, according to the preference which they may have for the stream, the plain, or the grove . . . They do not make use of stone cut from the quarry, or of tiles; for every kind of building they make use of unshapely wood, which falls short of beauty or attractiveness. They carefully colour some parts of their buildings with earth which is so clear and bright as to resemble painting and coloured designs.

At Warendorf, in Westphalia, German archaeologists have excavated some eighty buildings of an Anglo-Saxon village. Many of these were small outhouses, working sheds, barns, and cow sheds. Reconstructions of the various types of building found at Warendorf are illustrated in Fig. 6. The long house with the steeply-pitched roof at the top of the picture is typical of the dwelling houses that were found on the site. The ground plans and the remains of the walls of about six of these houses were found and from this it was possible to reconstruct the whole building. These long houses

Fig. 6   Reconstructions of different types of Saxon
buildings at Warendorf, Germany

varied in length between 42 and 87 feet and were the
most important type of building found on the site. We
must presume that the Anglo-Saxon farmer lived in
such a building with his family. The serfs and servants
apparently lived in smaller houses of the types shown
in Fig. 6, 2, 3, and 5. But many outhouses were used to
sleep in and we can imagine the weaving women
sleeping in the weaving shed that was excavated by
Mr. Leeds at Sutton Courtenay, Berkshire, which like
house No. 5 in Fig. 6, was partly sunk into the ground.

The houses, as Tacitus wrote, were constructed of
wood. Over a frame like that illustrated in Fig. 7 were
laid either overlapping planks or wattle hurdles
covered with mud daub, which may have been, as
Tacitus says, coloured. The roofs were presumably
covered with thatch, although there is some evidence
that in the larger houses wooden shingles were used.

There were many varieties of house in the Anglo-
Saxon period, some had stone foundations, and some
may even have had stone walls, but in general outward
appearance most of them would look rather like the
houses from Warendorf illustrated in Fig. 6. In some
of the houses both the animals and the humans would
live side by side, separated only by a low wall or a thin
wooden or wattle screen. The fire would be in the
centre of the floor and there was probably a hole in the
roof to allow the smoke to escape, but in the depths of a
cold winter, or when it rained, the hole would be
closed and the smoke would be left to find its own way
out through the various chinks and cracks that must
have abounded in these roughly built houses. The
cooking was done over this fire and the food was served
to the members of the household who would eat it
sitting on the floor or on benches running along the
sides of the house. In the poorer houses the whole

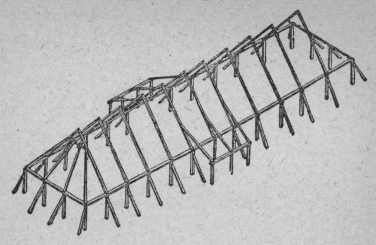

Fig. 7   Reconstruction of frame-work of a house from Warendorf

family would sleep in the same room, warmed by the dying embers of the central fire.

Having dealt with the house, and how it was built,

Fig. 8   Construction of wall and roof of timber-framed house

we will discuss the table furniture of the Anglo-Saxons. Each man carried his own knife. Fig. 9 shows one of these, from a burial, where it had been placed for the use of its owner in the spirit world. Spoons and forks were extremely rare and would only be owned by the rich, and even the rich would use only a knife at table.

The table glass was very beautiful; not a clear

white, but in ambers, blues, and greens, decorated in a very glass-blowing way with tears, or gouts (Fig. 10) of the molten glass, which being hollow, are in some miraculous way connected with the inside so that the wine could flow into them.

Fig. 9 Urn with implements found in it (*British Museum*)

Others have spidery threads laid on. Often they had no foot to stand on, and the contents had to be tossed off at a draught. Fig. 4 shows one of these. Other patterns are shown in Figs. 10 and 11.

Pottery of course was made, and Figs. 9 and 14 show cinerary urns. Fig. 13 shows a rare jug from the British Museum, dating from the fifth century. Its handle is perforated as a spout. Fig. 12 shows a bottle of reddish ware. This is Jutish, and the Jutes' pottery, like their jewellery, was different from that of the Angles and Saxons. In the early part of the Anglo-Saxon period the pottery was hand-made, and it was not until the eighth century that wheel-turned pottery was re-introduced into England. There is one exception to this rule; in Kentish Anglo-Saxon graves a reddish wheel-turned pottery is found. But this may have been imported from the Low Countries.

Fig. 10 Anglo-Saxon glass (*British Museum*)

The houses were lighted by candles, rush lights, or oil-burning lamps. William of Malmesbury tells how when Ethelred II was a boy of 10 years old,

Fig. 11 Anglo-Saxon glass
(*British Museum*)

he so irritated his furious mother by his weeping, that not having a whip at hand, she beat the little innocent with some candles she had snatched up . . . on this account he dreaded candles during the rest of his life.

When we turn to the personal belongings of the Anglo-Saxons, we shall have to study these in connection with their burials. This may sound a little dismal, but all the everyday things we possess of the period have been found in graves. With one exception (at Sutton Courtenay, which is not very helpful), there is no site which can be instanced as Anglo-Saxon, in the way that Silchester can be of Roman Britain.

Graves, however, are a wonderful indication of the outlook of a people. The heathen sometimes burned his dead, and buried arms and implements with the ashes, for use in the spirit world. In doing this, he was more helpful to the archaeologist than the Christian, who was buried, to await the Resurrection, without any such aids.

From the Old Stone Age we have traced how the changes

Fig. 12 Jutish bottle
(*British Museum*)

were rung through the centuries, between burial by burning – cremation – and by interring the unburned body in the earth, called inhumation. At the end of the Roman period inhumation became general. This was altered once more because some Saxons burned their dead. Fig. 14 shows one of the cinerary urns from the British Museum. These are grey, brown, or black and, what is very extra-

Fig. 13 Anglo-Saxon jug
(*British Museum*)

ordinary, they are not turned on a wheel but are hand-made, like the prehistoric pottery described in *Prehistoric Times*. Cremation seems to have appealed very especially to the Anglians, and was retained longer by them than by the Saxons. The Jutes always favoured inhumation.

Fig. 9 shows a cinerary urn from the British Museum with the implements which were buried with the ashes. Smaller pots perhaps contained food and drink for use on the journey to the other world. In the British Museum can be seen the contents of a grave of a chieftain at Taplow. This was dug 12 feet long, by 8 feet wide, by 6 feet deep, and east to west, but the head was at the east, instead of at the

Fig. 14 A Pagan burial urn
(*British Museum*)

west, as in Christian usage. The spear lay inverted at the side of the skeleton and the sword was placed ready to hand. The gold buckle, and clasps of the belt, are very beautiful, set with garnets and lapis lazuli. Above the head were two shields, an iron knife and ring. To the south-east were a bucket and bronze bowl. There were glass cups, and the remains of a large tub which had been placed over the thighs of the warrior. Two drinking horns (Fig. 15) were there to quench his thirst, and thirty bone draughtsmen accompanied him to while away the time. There is another set at the British Museum made from horses' teeth.

The grave at Taplow was covered with a barrow or mound of earth, and its furniture gives us a very good idea of the belongings of a chieftain. Heathen burials ceased with the final conversion of the English by Wilfrid about 681. Tombstones were used in later Saxon times.

In the summer of 1939 there was dug from British soil one of the richest treasures it can ever have contained. This was the celebrated Sutton Hoo treasure, the greatest single find known to British archaeology.

A Saxon sea-going ship, eighty foot long, was found beneath a barrow on a sandy heath near the Suffolk coast. The barrow was one of a small compact group of barrows situated on the bank of the River Deben, opposite the town of Woodbridge, about ten miles from Ipswich. Three or four hundred years ago grave-robbers had attempted to plunder the barrow, and the hole they dug into it from the top was still visible. The robbers had missed the centre of the ship, where the marvellous treasure lay, by a matter of inches.

The professional archaeologists who excavated the barrow in 1939 used very different methods from those of the fly-by-night bunglers who had sought mere loot. Their work ranks among the most careful and systematic excavations ever undertaken. It seems almost incredible, but the little band of scholars went about their work with such patient thoroughness that they laid bare the entire outline of the ancient Saxon vessel, despite the fact that its timbers had long since rotted away. All they had to guide them were the iron clench-nails which once held the planks together, and a dark stain in the sand where the wood had been. With these meagre clues they reconstructed the original appearance of the once proud ship, an early relative of the Gokstad ship (Fig. 31). Unlike the Gokstad ship and other Viking ships, the Sutton Hoo ship does not appear to have had a sail. Instead, it was rowed along by a crew of thirty-eight oarsmen.

In the centre of the ship the Saxon burial-party had erected a wooden cabin. They then strewed bracken over it, and heaped above it an oval mound of earth faced with turf. In the cabin were deposited the personal effects of the powerful chieftain in whose honour the ship had been dragged from the estuary to its resting-place on the upland heath. There was the chieftain's iron standard, over six foot high and topped with the emblem of a stag. There was a huge ceremonial whetstone, near which lay the great sword it may once have sharpened. The blade was rusted for ever in its leather scabbard, but the hilt still gleamed with gold and rich jewels. There were the remains of the big shield the warrior bore on his left arm, and also the

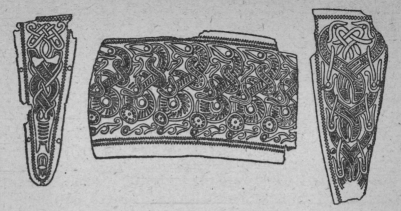

Fig. 16 Designs on the silver mounts of drinking-horns dug from a barrow at Sutton Hoo, Suffolk, in 1939 (*British Museum*)

crushed remnants of his fine helmet, ornamented with bronze and silver plaques and provided with projecting pieces to protect his ears and neck. To the front of the helmet was fixed a fearsome-looking mask, a hinged vizor worked in silver, bronze, and garnet, to shield the wearer's face. Near by were the chieftain's throwing-axe, and his hawberk, or coat of mail.

There were objects in profusion: iron spears, cauldrons and buckets, bronze bowls, and silver drinking-horns. Beneath a great silver dish, bearing the imperial stamp of Anastasius I of Byzantium, was a fluted silver bowl with the head of a classical goddess in the centre. Near a set of nine shallow silver bowls lay two silver spoons, each ten inches in length, with the names 'Paulos' and 'Saulos' engraved on them in Greek characters, symbols no doubt of some ancient christening ceremony.

Even these splendid trophies do not exhaust the total of the discoveries made at Sutton Hoo. For the most magnificent pieces of all are unquestionably the jewels, scattered in profusion among the effects of the dead leader. They were given by their owner, Mrs. Pretty, to the British Museum, where they are now displayed. All the gold pieces except the great belt-buckle are jewelled with garnets, a beautiful deep red semi-precious stone, and there are over four thousand tiny pieces of garnet in the whole collection of jewellery, each one cut individually to fit snugly into its little golden pit. From among the many buckles and clasps and mounts and buttons we may single out the purse-lid, enriched with plaques once set in a base of ivory or bone. The purse contained thirty-seven gold coins, and its catch and hinges, like those of all the other jewellery, still work perfectly after thirteen centuries at the bottom of the earthen barrow. The intricate patterns on the objects from Sutton Hoo, so savage yet so sophisticated, merit a special study. The weird birds and animals and reptiles are twisted and contorted into a hundred subtle shapes. It must be apparent to everyone who sees these specimens of their handiwork that the Saxon craftsmen were not only gifted metal-workers but superb artists as well.

The Sutton Hoo barrow is not a burial but a ceno-taph, a monument to a soldier who died fighting and whose remains were not recovered by his followers, for no body was found in the barrow. The notion that the grave is a cenotaph happens to agree, as it falls out, with the strongest candidature for the monument. It would seem that we have at Sutton Hoo a token burial of a king of East Anglia called Aethelhere, who was drowned by a flood on the battlefield of Winwaed in Yorkshire. Aethelhere had allied himself with the pagan King Penda of Mercia against Christian North-umbria, and the disastrous fight at Winwaed, described by the Venerable Bede, took place in A.D. 655.

At present the authorities incline to the opinion that Aethelhere's court trappings were buried at Sutton Hoo, as a token of respect, by his followers. We thus have at Sutton Hoo a particularly sumptuous example of the lavish funerals accorded to pagan monarchs, one of the last of its kind ever undertaken in Britain.

The practice of medicine in Anglo-Saxon times seem to have consisted of faith healing, assisted by rough surgery. In 660, the physician Cynefrid operated on Queen Etheldrida, who had 'a very great swelling under her jaw'. 'And I was ordered', said he, 'to lay open that swelling, to let out the noxious matter in it.'

Again in 698, the surgeons were puzzled by a youth whose eyelid had a great swelling on it. They 'applied their medicines to ripen it, but in vain. Some said it ought to be cut off; others opposed it, for fear of worse consequences.'

Bleeding was a popular cure for many diseases. One young girl who was very ill was bled in the arm. A bishop was asked to help, but said,

You did very indiscreetly and unskilfully to bleed her in the fourth day of the moon; for I remember that Archbishop Theodore, of blessed memory, said that bleeding at that time was very dangerous, when the light of the moon and the tide of the ocean is increasing; and what can I do to the girl if she is like to die?

Matters were not arranged very cheerfully for the patients. An earl's servant had lost the use of all his limbs, and again a bishop was called in and 'saw him in a dying condition, and the coffin at his side'.

Bede writes, 'a sudden pestilence (664) also depopulated the southern coasts of Britain, and afterwards extending into the province of the Northumbrians, ravaged the country far and near, and destroyed a great multitude of men'. These plagues recurred through the centuries, and were caused by lack of knowledge of hygiene and the fouling of the water supply. The jointed drain pipes of Mycenae, and the uses of the sewers of Roman Britain were forgotten.

The Church in Saxon times introduced the practice of burying within the sacred building. Bede wrote of another practice which the doctors of today would hardly recommend. St. Chad was buried and

the place of the sepulchre is a wooden monument, made like a little house, covered, having a hole in the wall, through which those that go thither for devotion usually put in their hand and take out some dust, which they put into water and give to sick cattle or men to drink, upon which they are presently eased of their infirmity, and restored to health.

However, we shall have a totally wrong idea of the Anglo-Saxons, if we think of them as ignorant barbarians. At the end of our first period, in 781, before the Danes had wasted the country, Alcuin, a Northumbrian educated at York, went to the Court of Charlemagne and gave him a thorough knowledge of logic, rhetoric, and astronomy. The man who was governing all Western Europe, with the exception of Spain, turned to England for instruction. This is not surprising when we consider that at this period England was a storehouse of knowledge; York, for example, before it was sacked by the Vikings, had the largest library north of the Alps.

Bede tells us that, as early as 635, King Sigebert

being desirous to imitate the good institutions which
he had seen in France, he set up a school for youth
(at Seaham or Dunwich) to be instructed in literature. [Theodore (699) assisted by Hadrian] gathered
a crowd of disciples . . . and, together with the books
of holy writ, they also taught them the arts of
ecclesiastical poetry, astronomy, and arithmetic. A
testimony of which is, that there are still living at this
day some of their scholars, who are as well versed in
the Greek and Latin tongues as in their own.

Children started their schooling at an early age.
Bede wrote of a boy, Esica, not above three years old,
placed in a monastery to pursue his studies.

We do not hear much about games in Saxon times,
perhaps because life was so interesting that it was more
amusing to play at being grown up, with romps in
between, as the Eskimo children do today. They have
small weapons and implements and learn their job by
playing at it. Small Saxon battle-axes have been found
which suggest this. Here is a note on horse racing.

We came into a plain and open road, well adapted
for galloping our horses. The young men that were
with him and particularly those of the laity, began
to entreat the bishop to give them leave to gallop,
and make trial of the goodness of their horses.

Chess was played, as was some form of draughts.

Bede was not only the first of the English historians,
but a classical scholar as well. He referred to Plato's
'Republic' when he wrote: 'a certain worldly writer

Fig. 17   Saxon initials

most truly said, that the world would be most happy if either kings were philosophers, or philosophers were kings'.

It was in a monastery at Whitby, that Caedmon, one of the lay brothers, first received inspiration, and became the father of English poetry.

Gildas, who has been called the British Jeremiah, wrote his history as early as 545. It might have been of supreme interest, but, unfortunately for us, the book, starting as a history, very speedily develops into a moral lecture. Gildas has hardly a good word to say for the Britons, who were delivered into the hands of the Saxons because of their sins; then the turn of the Saxons comes, and they are denounced as being 'a race hateful both to God and man'. Gildas has one interesting reference to the 'diabolical idols ... of which we still see some mouldering away within or without the deserted temples, with stiff and deformed features as was customary.' As he refers also to walled towns, these architectural remains must have been survivals of Romano-British building.

Geoffrey of Monmouth lived much later, between 1100–54. He must have been a delightful person. One phrase gives a taste of his quality: 'The island was then called Albion and was inhabited by none but a few giants.' As we have not yet interested ourselves in the everyday life of giants we have not drawn on Geoffrey for information. He wrote, or, as he himself says, translated into Latin, a very ancient book of British History. He did this because neither Gildas nor Bede said anything 'of those kings who lived here before the Incarnation of Christ, nor of Arthur'. Bede probably doubted the authenticity of their figures, and we suspect that the 'ancient book' existed only in Geoffrey's imagination. What he did was to gather all the legends

together, to serve the very useful purpose of being the fountain head from
which the poets and writers of romance
drew their inspiration. There are hap-
penings in Greece and Rome, and
Gaul and Britain. Leir and Cordeilla,
Merlin and the magicians and Arthur
all live in his pages.

Fig. 18 Figure
from the Book
of Kells

We must now consider Manuscripts,
because these writings on vellum were
the means by which the literature of the time was given
to the people.

The Anglo-Saxons were skilled penmen and artists;
many of the beautiful manuscripts which they produced survive to this day. Books were
precious objects, written by hand and
illuminated by drawings which often
have little or no relationship to the text
but which merely enrich and beautify
the pages. The first letters of a para-
graph, for example, might be contorted
and twisted and perhaps embellished
with a small animal head. A particularly
magnificent initial X almost completely
fills the page of one manuscript and a
series of small, yet delightful, initials are
illustrated in Fig. 17. Sometimes, as in
Fig. 18, the artist attempted to draw
human and animal figures and, although
he may not seem to have been very
successful in representing them directly,
he often caught the spirit of the fabulous
animal he was portraying.

Fig. 19 Figure
from the
Gospels of
St. Chad

Nobody knows when manuscripts
were first painted in England, but as

Fig. 20   David rescuing the lamb from the lion (*From a Psalter in St. John's College, Cambridge*)

most writing was done by clerics we must presume that the introduction of Christianity at the end of the sixth century was responsible for the start of English writing and painting. But the earliest manuscript written in the British Isles that survives must date from about the middle of the seventh century. One of the finest works of art ever produced in this country was written and illuminated about fifty years later. It takes its name from the monastery in which it was made and is known as the Lindisfarne Gospels. The quality of the penmanship used in illuminating this book is so extremely fine that a modern artist would probably not be able to equal it. The brilliant colours of the interlaced animal ornament are an impressive testimony to the skill of the Anglo-Saxon artist.

The tradition of fine illumination never completely died out in England, although during Alfred's reign and in the difficult years that followed few manuscripts survive which are of very great quality. It was in this period that the practice of outline drawing was introduced into England from the Continent. This practice developed alongside the native tradition of fine coloured illumination throughout the tenth century. The English tradition of

Fig. 21   A border from the Gospels of Durrow

Fig. 22 The back of Franks casket, carved in whale's bone. Northumbrian work, *c.* A.D. 700 (*British Museum*)

Fig. 23 Reconstructed
bone writing-tablet
from Blythburgh,
Suffolk
(*British Museum*)

manuscript illumination can be seen to reach a new peak in the tenth century with the production of two important books (now in the British Museum): the Benedictional of St. Aethelwold and the Charter of the New Minster at Winchester. That this tradition continued in the period after the Norman Conquest can be seen from a group of manuscripts produced at Durham in the late eleventh century which are in direct descent from the earlier English manuscripts.

We have seen, on page 28, that Bede stated how, by the study of Scripture, the Latin tongue, and with it Roman characters, become common to the people; but there were others. A scramasax, or knife, at the British Museum is interesting because it has the Runic characters engraved on it. This system of writing was used by the Nordic peoples, and dates back to the fourth century, but was not in general use in England after the eighth. Its angular form made it very suitable for engraving on wood or stone.

Runes are cut on the wonderful Franks casket in the King Edward VII Gallery at the British Museum, Fig. 22, to explain the carvings, where Egil the archer is shown fighting his enemies; Wayland the smith makes a drinking-cup of a skull, and Romulus

Fig. 24 Bronze seal
of Ethilwald, Bishop
of Dunwich, about
850, from Eye, Suffolk (*British Museum*)

and Remus are with their foster-mother the Wolf. The casket is made of whalebone, and is Northumbrian work of about A.D. 700. It should be studied also for the details it gives of costume.

Another form of writing is that which employed the Ogham characters. These can be studied at the British Museum, and consisted of horizontal and diagonal strokes, and dots, grouped in series up to five, cut on the faces and edges of a tombstone for example. It is thought that the system was invented in Ireland.

The British Museum contains the only known example of a tenth century Anglo-Saxon writing-tablet Fig. 23 made of bone with sunk panels inside in which wax was spread to take the scratched writing done with a metal stylus.

Other writing was done with a reed, or quill pen, on the parchment of manuscripts or deeds. These were sealed with wax, by a bronze seal Fig. 24 which belonged to Ethilwald, Bishop of Dunwich, whose See, or seat, had long since been swallowed up by the waves.

At the Museum there is an impression of a seal, in lead, of Coenwulf, king of Mercia, 796–819. It was a *bulla* of lead like this, attached to papal documents, which gave rise to the name of papal 'bulls'.

We will consider now the great part which Christianity played in civilizing the English, but first we must endeavour to put ourselves in their places. We must remember that their faith had been much the same as that of the Vikings we describe on page 80, and an eminently suitable one for the warrior. By fighting he reached Valhal, and remained there. There were no complexities, or subtleties; the gods were destroyers like men. We must try and imagine their astonishment when Aidan, or Augustine, preached to them of the

Sermon on the Mount, and told them that men were made in the image of God, and not a god like Woden, but a God of Love; that they could be creators. Here was a Faith which was easy to understand, and yet so difficult to live up to, because men continued, and still continue, to be more like the images of the old heathen gods they themselves had made.

We will trace all this in the pages of Bede, but first we must remember, as already stated on page 15, that the Britons were converted long before the Mission of St. Augustine, and that the Irish Church was in continuous descent from the Romano-British Church. There were differences between the Church of Ireland and that of Rome, mainly as to the proper date for keeping Easter, and these were not composed until the Synod of Whitby in 664. We must not think of Rome as the only source of Christian inspiration. When Christ was born, Rome, and Roman civilization, was at a low ebb, and it was not till the Edict of Toleration, in 313, that Christianity was recognized there. But Christ was born in Palestine, and here it was in Asia Minor that the greater part of the work of the Apostles was carried out. As a result, Christianity was adopted as the State religion at Edessa, in North Mesopotamia, as early as 202, and in Armenia at the end of the century. Bede, in the first chapter of his history, compares England with Armenia, Macedonia, Italy, and other countries. This is very interesting, because Professor Strzygowski has shown that there are striking parallels between the church architecture of Asia Minor and that evolved here in England. The church at Silchester built here in Roman times can be called Basilican, because it was founded on the Roman basilica, and the Saxon church of Worth, in Sussex, follows the same pattern and has an apse at the east end. If, however, we take Escomb,

Fig. 25   Old timber-framed church at Urnes, Sogn,
Norway. Eleventh century

Durham, we find a different type of church with a
square ended chancel. This latter type may have been
introduced, not from Rome, but Asia Minor, and it is
more usual in England than the apse. The question is
were they influenced in their design by motives which
travelled from Asia Minor to South Russia in the same
way as the love of colour and jewellery to which we
referred on page 17. Many of the Saxon churches
give the idea of timber designs carried out in stone and
they brought a timber building tradition with them.

Some of the early churches must have been on the
lines of the old Norwegian timber church Fig. 25. We
deal more fully with church architecture in the next
chapter.

The practice of building wayside crosses seems to
have started in Saxon times. These marked the way, or

Fig. 26
Ornament,
Urnes Church

the parting of the ways, or where the river could be forded, or, as a nun writing in 699, said,

> it is customary among the Saxon people, on the estates of the nobles or gentry, to have for the use of those who make a point of attending daily prayers, not a church, but the sign of the Holy Cross, set up aloft and consecrated to the Lord.

Augustine came to England in 597, at the instigation of Bertha, daughter of the king of the Franks, and wife of Ethelbert, king of Kent. We shall let Bede tell the tale:

> On the east of Kent is the large Isle of Thanet, containing, according to the English way of reckoning, 600 families. [Augustine stayed until] Some days after, the king came into the island, and sitting in the open air, ordered Augustine and his companions to be brought into his presence. For he had taken precaution that they should not come to him in any house, lest, according to an ancient superstition, if they practised any magical arts, they might impose upon him, and so get the better of him.

As a result of his preaching, Augustine was allowed to settle at Canterbury, where

there was on the east side of the city, a church dedi-

cated to the honour of St. Martin, built whilst the
Romans were still in the island, wherein the queen,
who, as has been said before, was a Christian, used to
pray. In this they first began to meet, to sing, to
pray, to say mass, to preach and to baptize, till the
king, being converted to the faith, allowed them to
preach openly, and build or repair churches in all
places.

The Roman St. Martin's appears to have consisted
of a plain oblong chapel, with a semi-circular apse of
which little remains now, because the western end of
the present chancel was the eastern end of the original
chapel, and the apse lies under the floor where the
building has been extended. Bede shows that at the
time of Augustine, there must have been many other
Romano-British churches.

The sudden conversion of great multitudes of people
presented difficulty when they came to be baptized.
Baptism was by total immersion, and as Bede tells us,
'for as yet oratories, or fonts, could not be made in the
early infancy of the church in these parts', so the
grown-up converts flocked to the rivers and were baptized there.

One of the sites associated with Paulinus's mission
to Northumbria is Yeavering in Northumberland, a
place we described briefly on page 34. Here in 627 at
the request of King Edwin Paulinus spent a number of
days baptizing the people in the neighbourhood.

We can imagine Paulinus preaching to the pagans
and newly converted Christians from the rostrum of
the moot (or meeting-place), the plan of which was
uncovered by Mr. Hope-Taylor: it had a triangular
plan with a curved short side (not unlike a wedge of
cake) with a rostrum at the apex. The seats rose from

the rostrum in tiers so that the whole audience was able
to see the speaker clearly.

There is a beautiful passage in Bede, dealing with the
conversion of Edwin of Northumbria, in 625, by
Paulinus, who was

> tall of stature, a little stooping, his hair black, his
> visage meagre, his nose slender and aquiline, his
> aspect both venerable and majestic. [He preached
> to the king, and Coifi, the chief priest, urged that the
> old gods be deserted] For none of your people has
> applied himself more diligently to the worship of
> our gods than I; and yet there are many who receive
> greater favours from you, and are more preferred
> than I, and are more prosperous in all their under-
> takings. Now if the gods were good for anything they
> would rather forward me, who have been more care-
> ful to serve them.

Here is a splendid illustration of the old pagan spirit;
a bargain was made with the gods and, for the service
rendered by worship, rewards were expected.

Another of the king's chief men was moved by Paulinus to a nobler strain, and said:

> The present life of man, O king, seems to me, in
> comparison of that time which is unknown to us, like
> to the swift flight of a sparrow through the room
> wherein you sit at supper in winter, with your
> commanders and ministers, and a good fire in the
> midst, whilst the storms of rain and snow prevail
> abroad; the sparrow, I say, flying in at one door, and
> immediately out at another, whilst he is within is
> safe from the wintry storm; but after a short space
> of fair weather, he immediately vanishes out of your

sight, into the dark winter from which he had emerged. So this life of man appears for a short space, but of what went before, or what is to follow, we are utterly ignorant. If, therefore, this new doctrine contains something more certain, it seems justly to deserve to be followed.

This man was a poet.

Coifi, as a priest, could not carry arms and had to ride a mare, so when he threw off his allegiance to the old gods he begged for the king's stallion and arms, and girding on a sword and taking a spear, galloped to the temple and cast the spear into the temple and destroyed it; but then Coifi was not a poet, and this was just the ungrateful thing that a realist would do.

But all the temples were not destroyed in this way. Pope Gregory wrote to Abbot Mellitus, in 601, that

the temples of the idols in that nation (English) ought not to be destroyed; but let the idols that are in them be destroyed; let holy water be made and sprinkled in the said temples, let altars be erected and relics placed.

We have already seen how one of these pagan temples, at Yeavering, was adapted to Christian use (page 34).

Again the Church was charitable. Pope Gregory pointed out that as the heathen English had 'been used to slaughter many oxen in the sacrifices to devils, some solemnity must be exchanged for them on this account'. Christianity was not to be made doleful. The festivals were to be feast days when the people could be festive. They were to be allowed 'to build themselves huts of the boughs of trees, about those churches which have been turned to that use from temples, and celebrate the solemnity with religious feasting, and no more offer beasts to the Devil, but kill cattle to the praise of God in their eating'.

So the good work continued until it looked as if the country were to see peace. We read that in the time of Edwin, King of Northumbria, 'a woman with her new-born babe might walk throughout the island, from sea to sea, without receiving any harm. That king took such care for the good of his nation that in several places where he had seen clear springs near the high-ways he caused stakes to be fixed, with brass dishes hanging at them, for the convenience of travellers.' But the fight was not won yet. Edwin was killed at the battle of Hatfield, by invading Mercians under Penda, who was still pagan. Paulinus fled to the south, and his work was largely undone.

Now we come to the very special service which the Church of Ireland rendered to the Christian cause. Oswald, the king who succeeded to the throne of Northumbria, had passed some part of his youth in the monastery of Iona, which, as we have seen on page 18, was founded by Columba, who went there from Ireland about 563, and it was to Iona that Oswald sent for help. They sent him, in 635, 'Bishop Aidan, a man of singular meekness, piety, and moderation; zealous in the cause of God, though not altogether according to knowledge; for he was wont to keep Easter Sunday according to the custom of his country.' This was the old quarrel.

Oswald appointed Aidan to his episcopal see in the Isle of Lindisfarne, which we call Holy Island for this reason, and he was successful in his work of reconversion. We read in Bede that many religious men and women, stirred by the example of Aidan, 'adopted the custom of fasting on Wednesdays and Fridays, till the ninth hour, throughout the year, except during the fifty days after Easter'. Later on, in 664, the differences between the two churches were composed, and Theodore 'was the first archbishop whom all the English Church obeyed'.

The conversion of the South Saxons occurred at an even later date. Bede tells how Bishop Wilfrid went to Sussex, in 681, and found the inhabitants in great distress. He baptized 250 men and women slaves, and 'not only rescued them from the servitude of the Devil, but gave them their bodily liberty also, and exempted them from the yoke of human servitude'.

He had put heart into them. A dreadful famine ensued on three years drought, so that often

forty or fifty men, being spent with want, would go together to some precipice, or to the seashore, and there, hand in hand, perish by the fall, or be swallowed up by the waves. [This was while they were heathen, because on the very day the nation was baptized rain fell. The bishops not only saved their souls, but] taught them to get their food by fishing; for their sea and rivers abounded in fish, but the people had no skill to take them, except eels alone. The bishop's men having gathered eel-nets everywhere, cast them into the sea, and by the blessing of God took three hundred fishes of several sorts.

Wilfrid founded a monastery at Selsey, the Island of the Sea-Calf. Earlier there had been a small monastery of Irish monks at Bosham, 'but none of the natives cared either to follow their course of life, or hear their preaching'.

The early Church was tremendously concerned in

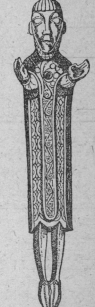

Fig. 27   Figure of
Christ, in
bronze. Irish
(*British Museum*)

keeping its members to the true
Faith, and it had to combat the
heretics who would have
divided it up into many
small sects. Had this happened, the assault on heathendom
would have failed, and with the
failure the history of Western
Europe would have been different.
The Greek Church, which is a federation of many eastern churches
of which the most important is the
Church of Russia, remained in communion with the Church of Rome
until 1054.

Again the Church
was compelled to interest itself in temporal affairs. The Popes wrote to the
Kings, and urged them to lead Christian
lives, and the Pope signed himself, 'the
servant of the servants of God'. Pope
Boniface, in 625, wrote to King Edwin,
and sent him 'a shirt, with one gold
ornament, and one garment of Ancyra',
and to Queen Ethelberga 'a silver looking-glass, and gilt-ivory comb'.

The bishops were rewarded. Pope
Gregory sent the pallium to Augustine.
The pallium was a long strip of fine
woollen cloth, ornamented with crosses,
the middle of which was formed with a
loose collar resting on the shoulders,
while the extremities before and behind
hung down nearly to the feet.

Fig. 28   Figure in
Bronze. Irish
(*British Museum*)

It would be well for us perhaps to try and catch a little of the spirit which animated these men in their fight, because it was as a fight against the powers of darkness that they regarded their work. If they held a Bible in one hand, in the other there was a sword.

Augustine summoned a conference, in 603, to which the bishops of the Britons were invited, and at which the date of Easter was discussed. Augustine wrought a miracle restoring a blind man's sight, after the British bishops had failed, to convince them that his church was in the right; but they remained unconvinced. Bede then tells how

the man of God, Augustine, is said, in a threatening manner, to have foretold, that in case they would not join in unity with their brethren, they should be warred upon by their enemies; and, if they would not preach the way of life to the English nation, they should at their hands undergo the vengeance of death.

This is what happened. The Britons were defeated by the English, at Chester, with great slaughter, and 1,200 monks from Bangor were among the slain. There was not much love lost between them. Even Bede refers to the Britons as 'that perfidious nation'.

Bede gives a beautiful vision of what the seventh-century man was given to expect after death. A Northumbrian rose from the dead, and related the things which he had seen.

He that led me had a shining countenance and a bright garment, and we went on silently, as I thought, towards the north-east. Walking on, we came to a vale of great breadth and depth, but of infinite length; on the left it appeared full of dreadful flames, the other side was no less horrid for violent hail and cold snow flying in all directions; both places were full of men's souls, which seemed by turns to be tossed from one side to the other, as it were by a violent storm; for when the wretches could no longer endure the excess of heat, they leaped into the middle of the cutting cold; and finding no rest there, they leaped back again into the middle of the unquenchable flames [the guide said] this is not the hell you imagine.

They passed on to a place where

As we went on through the shades of night, on a sudden there appeared before us frequent globes of black flames, rising as it were out of a great pit, and falling back again into the same. When I had been conducted thither, my leader suddenly vanished, and left me alone in the midst of darkness and this horrid vision, whilst those same globes of fire, without intermission, at one time flew up and at another fell back into the bottom of the abyss; and I observed that all the flames, as they ascended, were full of human souls, which, like sparks flying up with smoke were sometimes thrown on high, and again, when the vapour of the fire ceased, dropped down into the depth below.

Turning towards the south-east, and coming to the top of a vast wall, they found within it a delightful field, full of fragrant flowers. 'In this field were innumerable assemblies of men in white, and many companies seated together rejoicing.' The Northumbrian was told: 'This is not the kingdom of heaven, as you imagine.'

Fig. 29 The Ruthwell Cross (partial reconstruction). The cross is now
inside Ruthwell Church, Dumfriesshire

When he had passed farther on he

discovered before me a much more beautiful light, and therein heard sweet voices of people singing, and so wonderful a fragrancy proceeded from the place, that the other which I had before thought most delicious, then seemed to me very indifferent; even as that extraordinary brightness of the flowery field, compared with this, appeared mean and inconsiderable.

But beyond this they were not allowed to pass.

The guide then told the Northumbrian what were the places he had seen. The dreadful vale was the place 'in which the souls of those are tried and punished, who, delaying to confess their crimes, at length have recourse to repentance at the point of death', but after punishment they were received into the Kingdom of Heaven.

The fiery pit was the mouth of Hell, 'into which whosoever falls shall never be delivered to all eternity'.

The first flowery field was the place for those who were

not so perfect as to deserve to be immediately admitted into the Kingdom of Heaven; yet they shall all, at the day of judgment, see Christ, and partake of the joys of His kingdom; for whoever are perfect, in thought, word and deed, as soon as they depart the body, immediately enter into the Kingdom of Heaven; in the neighbourhood whereof that place is, where you heard the sound of sweet singing, with the fragrant odour and bright light.

2

THE COMING OF THE VIKINGS

SO far as this part is concerned, we shall deal with the
history of our country, between 815, when the Britons
were finally conquered by the Saxons under Ecgberht,
King of Wessex, up to the final conquest of the Saxons
by the Danes under Canute in 1016, and then on to the
Norman Invasion in 1066.

In the Saga of Burnt Njal is told the story of a
Viking warrior who joined forces with Hallvard the
White and went to seek his fortune away from his
family and homeland. The name of this warrior was
Gunnar and he was typical of many men from Scandinavia in the period between the eighth and eleventh
centuries. Gunnar and those like him were pirates and
their names indicate their character: Eric Bloodaxe,
Harold Wartooth, Wolf the Unwashed, and Thorkell
the Skull-splitter. They were tough pirates who plundered and burnt their way across Europe, from the
Mediterranean to the North Atlantic, from the Cas-
pian Sea to St. George's Channel, leaving a trail of
devastation in their wake.

It was not till 787 that the Vikings turned their
attention to this country. We read in the Anglo-Saxon
Chronicle, that in this year

first came three ships of Northmen, out of Haere-
thaland (Denmark). And then the reve (sheriff)

rode out to the place, and would have driven them
to the King's town, because he knew not who they
were: and they there slew him. These were the first
ships of Danishmen who sought the land of the
English nation.

'God's church at Lindisfarne' was destroyed in 793,
and Jarrow 794. There appear to have been two lines
of attack. The first was from the Danes and Gotas who
lived around the Wick, or Vik, now the fjord of Oslo.
A glance at the map will show how easily they could
come south by hugging the shore, and then crossing to
the Thames, work down the Channel. The second line
was from Norway to Shetland, and then south on either
side of Scotland, to Northumbria on one hand, and
Ireland on the other.

The Vikings occupied Ireland for about two centuries, and were differentiated there, because the Norsemen were known as the white strangers (*Finn-Gaill*),
and the Danes as the dark strangers (*Dubh-Gaill*).

We know all these things; they are the common-
places of history. What we do not really understand is
how it came about that this Northern people should in
the first place have felt the tremendous necessity for
movement, and then have been so well equipped that
they were able to carry out their schemes.

There were probably many reasons why the Vikings
left their homeland in Scandinavia and went plunder-
ing in all parts of the known world. Some went out as
pirates for the simple reason that they wanted money,
some went in search of land, some to escape the law, or
the displeasure of the King, and some because they
were adventurers and were restless. Some went as
traders and the great ports of the Viking world –
Birka, near the modern Stockholm; Hedeby, near the

modern Slesvig; Shiringshal, near the modern Kaupang in Norway – were important merchant centres as well as meeting-places for the Viking pirates. And although there can be little doubt as to the rapacious character of the Vikings, it is well to remember that their doings were recorded by their enemies in extremely unfavourable terms and that it was the Vikings who introduced the word 'Law' into the English language.

Three ships came in 787, but in 833 as many as 35 came to Charmouth and, by 851, 350 came to the mouth of the Thames. We cannot follow all their movements here, but Wales, Ireland, and France were all raided. One important detail is that Rurik, King of Sweden, founded the kingdom of Russia at the end of the ninth century. In this way the Vikings reached Kief, and from here went to take service with the Emperor at Constantinople, and fought in Asia Minor against the Saracens.

Harald Sigurdsson, son of Sigurd Syr, King of Norway, did this, and later became King of Norway as Harald Haardraada. Always something seems to happen when the Northern peoples rub shoulders with the old civilizations of the Near East. The Vikings brought back with them the rarest of commodities, ideas, and we have to admit that they were an extraordinary people.

Roman power was based on the legionary, but the Viking was the first to realize the meaning of sea-power. Their ships were beautifully designed and very speedy, so when they sailed up the rivers conveniently arranged for them on our East Coast, they took horses, put their webbed feet in stirrups, and rode through the country. They were like evil will-o'-the-wisps, never where the Saxons expected to find them. The English ceorl, called up by the fyrd of the shire, was thinking of his crops, and armed only with spear and shield, was opposed to the Viking with steel cap and ring-mail shirt, who, as a mounted infantry man, could deliver his blow when, and where he liked.

This will be a good place in which to write of the Viking ship. If we turn back the pages of history we find how often some new idea has revolutionized the lives and liberties of the peoples. Armour, the bow, horse, military engineering, and the walled city, were all used in warfare long before the days of Christ. The Vikings had the wonderful ship which the stormy waters and the seafaring genius of their people had developed to perfection. We know what these were like, because the old Vikings loved their boats so well that they were buried in them. We saw on page 30 how in *Beowulf* the dead Scyld was placed in his ship, and pushed off to sail away into the unknown. In another type of funeral the body was placed in the ship and both burned together. A third type is more useful to the archaeologists, because here the ship was pulled up on to land, and the dead body placed in it, with all the articles which the warrior would need in the spirit world. Then over the whole a barrow of earth was piled to remain for excavation in our time.

It was a beautiful idea and shows how the Viking loved his ship: in the Sagas he calls it the 'Reindeer of the breezes', the 'Horse of gull's track', the 'Raven of the wind', and many other equally poetic names.

Shall we conjure up the burial scene? The ship drawn up, its prow pointing to the sea; a salt breeze blowing in, stinging the nostrils and singing in the rigging. The procession from the hall, the dead Viking borne by his warriors, the body stiff and cold but

Fig. 30   On board the Gokstad ship

dressed and armed for his last voyage. Then the
slaughter of the terrified horses and whimpering dogs
who were to accompany their master. Overhead,
attracted by the smell of blood, the wheeling, scream-
ing gulls, like valkyries sent by Odin as an escort to
Valhalla. Some such scene was staged around the ship
illustrated in Figs. 30 and 31. These illustrations have
been drawn from the boat discovered at Gokstad,
near Sandefjord on Oslofjord in Norway.

The ship was clinker built, with overlapping planks
of oak. About 78 feet long, her beam was 16 feet 7
inches, and depth 6 feet 9 inches. She had more beam
than is generally imagined (Fig. 31). The one square
sail was useful before the wind, and at other times
there were sixteen oars for pulling on each side. The
mast was stepped as shown in Fig. 30, and kept in
position by a heavy slab dropped into a slot; it was
lowered aft by slacking off the forestay. The vessel was
steered by an oar at a point near the stern. The lines

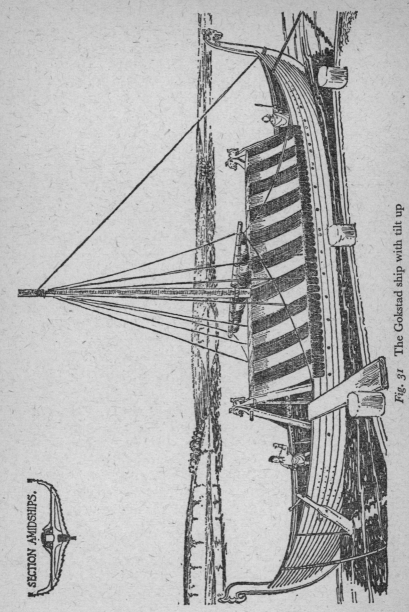

Fig. 31 The Gokstad ship with tilt up

SECTION AMIDSHIPS.

of hull were as beautiful as those of a modern yacht, and just as scientifically modelled, so as to offer the minimum resistance to the passage through the water. At night a tilt was put up (Fig. 31). Fig. 32 shows one

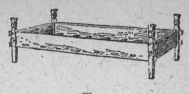

Fig. 32
A bed from the Gokstad ship

of the wooden beds found on the Gokstad ship. Made of oak, it is ingeniously constructed so that it could be taken to pieces. The posts are 2 feet 3 inches high; the ends 3 feet 5 inches wide, and the sides 7 feet 5 inches long. Only the chiefs would have had beds. Another Viking boat was recovered from Oseberg, not far from Gokstad. This was the burial ship of a queen and contained finely carved furniture and many implements and ornaments, some of which had been brought by the Vikings from England.

There is a note in William of Malmesbury bearing on boats. Godwin gave Hardicanute.

a ship beaked with gold, having eighty soldiers on board, who had two bracelets on either arm, each weighing sixteen ounces of gold; on their heads were gilt helmets; on their left shoulder they carried a Danish axe, with an iron spear in their right hand.

The Anglo-Saxon Chronicle (891) gives details of other boats in use at the time of far more primitive build – 'And three Scots (Irish) came to King Alfred in a boat without any oars from Ireland, whence they had stolen away. ... The boat in which they came was made of two hides and a half.' This sounds like a sea curragh made of wicker and covered with hide as the coracle. The curragh is still in use on the west coast of Ireland. Tarred canvas on a light wooden

frame replaces the animal skin. A rounder, smaller
kind is used by fishermen on Welsh rivers.

We can now return to the doings of the Vikings on
land. Asser tells a tale which shows that the Saxons
credited them with supernatural powers.

> They say, moreover, that in every battle, where-
> ever that flag went before them, if they were to gain
> the victory a live crow would appear flying in the
> middle of the flag; but if they were doomed to be
> defeated it would hang down motionless, and this
> was often proved so.

When they came to settle in the land, after the
Peace of Wedmore, in 878, they showed great judg-
ment in the selection of their five strongholds or burgs.
The Vikings knew the importance of transport and
they selected points which could easily be reached by
land or water. Lincoln was on the River Witham, at
the junction of the Roman Fosse Way and Ermine
Street; Stamford on Ermine Street, and the River
Welland; Leicester on the Fosse Way, and the River
Soar; Derby on the River Derwent, and Ryknield
Street; and Nottingham on the Trent.

When the Vikings were established in the Danelaw,
they doubtless sent for their wives and children, and
settled to live peacefully in the fortified towns of their
new country. The peaceful side of Viking life is
indicated by the comb illustrated in Fig. 9. A runic
inscription is scratched on the comb which reads in
the language and letters of a Viking 'Thorfastr made a
good comb'. But the Viking influence is most clearly
to be seen in our language and in our place-names. We
have already noticed that the word 'law' is Scandinavian in origin and many Norse survivals are to be found

in the dialects of Cumberland and Westmorland. To berry (*berja*, thresh); the boose (*báss*, cow-shed); galt (*galti*, a pig); garn (*garn*, yarn); handsel (*handsöl*, bargain), and many others. Similarly the termination -*by* to a place-name (as in Derby) is a sure sign that it was once a Viking settlement.

Where the Vikings settled, the land was divided into trithings, wapentakes, and carucates. In Domesday these measurements are applied to Nottingham, Leicester, Derby, Rutland, and Lincoln. Twelve carucates equal one hundred. The duodecimal, 12, seems to have come from the Dane, and the long hundred of 120 is a survival from their times. Another interesting detail is found in Domesday, where more freemen are mentioned in the Danelaw than elsewhere, and the men of that part still perhaps think of themselves as being sturdier in thought and action than their Saxon cousins of the South.

The names of the Things, or Assemblies, of which we read in Burnt Njal, survive in names, like the Suffolk hundred of Thingoe, or Tinghowe, Tingewick, near Buckingham, and Tingrith, South Bedfordshire.

But if the arrival of the Vikings was an advantage in one way, in that it stiffened the fibre of the race, in another it was fraught with great peril. When they first came, in 787, they were pagans and the delicate fabric of Christianity was torn down and trampled in the dust. Churches were destroyed, monasteries plundered, and the civilization of the country put back centuries.

Odin, Thor, and Frey were the greatest of their gods. Odin, the God of Wisdom, was the chief, and the same as the Anglo-Saxon Woden. Tall and bearded, he loved war, and his two ravens, Hugin and Munin,

Fig. 33   Font in Deerhurst Church, Gloucestershire. When set up again in the church the ornament of the base was placed immediately under the bowl

brought him news of men. He had only one eye, having sacrificed the other to drink wisdom at the Well of Mimir. As the Chief of the gods he had a hall, Valhal. The Valkyries were his attendants, and the choosers of the dead. Virgin goddesses, armed with helmet, shield and spear, and mounted on horseback, they rode through the air, over the rainbow, the celestial bridge which gods and men must tread to reach Valhalla. Only those who died in battle or who met a violent death were chosen, and taken to feast with Odin, to find their pastime in fighting and their reward in that they always lived on to feast, and fight, another day. The sorry souls who died in their beds never reached Valhal, but went instead to *Hel.* Ty was the God of War, and Thor, the Thunder God, protected farmers and threw his hammer, which is the thunder-bolt. The gods accepted the sacrifice of horses, oxen, sheep, and boars, but in times of great trouble their will was found by casting lots, and men were killed to appease them. This was the animating faith of the Vikings, who nearly conquered the world of their day, and whose blood still flows in English veins.

This period was a tragic one for the Saxons in England, the gloom of which was only dispelled by the gallant stand made by Alfred. He turned his levy into a militia, part of which was always on duty; he fortified burgs and improved his fleet. He not only protected England in his time, but laid the foundations of a power which was to conquer her yet again in 1066. Some Vikings finding that Alfred's fleet really did mean business, turned their attention to Gaul, where they eventually settled down, in 912, founding Normandy.

The Franks did not find them particularly pleasant neighbours. William of Malmesbury tells how Charles,

King of the Franks, finding that he could not beat the Normans, proposed to them that they should hold the land they had already conquered as his vassals. Rollo thought it over, and

the inbred and untamed ferocity of the man may well be imagined, for, on receiving this gift, as the bystanders suggested to him that he ought to kiss the foot of his benefactor, disdaining to kneel down, he seized the king's foot and dragged it to his mouth as he stood erect. The king falling on his back, the Normans began to laugh, and the Franks to be indignant.

This is an interesting passage. History was repeating itself. Long years before, the Franks and Saxons had descended on the Gauls and Britons and treated them in much the same way; now they themselves were helpless before the Vikings. Just as the Gauls and Britons had learned to lean on the strong arm of Rome, could not stand alone when it was withdrawn, so the Franks and Saxons found civilized life enervating.

We do not concern ourselves very much with the doings of kings, because generally they are so remote from everyday life, but this cannot be said of Alfred; perhaps that is why his name lives. Here was a king who, though kingly, had touched adversity and known trouble.

There are two tales which are well known, but explain why he had such a hold on his people. Asser tells one, of how when the king had taken refuge in a hut

it happened on a certain day, that the country-woman, wife of the cowherd, was preparing some loaves to bake, and the king, sitting at the hearth, made ready his bow and other warlike instruments. The unlucky woman espying the cakes burning at the fire, ran up to remove them,

and gave the king a little bit of her mind, telling him that if he wanted to eat the cakes, he might at least have watched them.

The other tale is told by William of Malmesbury, of the time when Alfred was hard pressed at Athelney:

Not long after, venturing from his concealment, he hazarded an experiment of consummate art. Accompanied only by one of his most faithful adherents, he entered the tent of the Danish king under the disguise of a minstrel; and being admitted, as a professor of the mimic art, to the banqueting room there was no object of secrecy that he did not minutely attend to, both with eyes and ears.

These are typical legends of a type that commonly grows up around a great hero; they should not be taken too literally – they are however indicative of the honour and affection in which Alfred was held by the English.

But even Alfred's genius could only maintain a hold on the south-west of England, and by the Peace of Wedmore, 878, Northumbria, half of Mercia, and East Anglia became the Danelaw. We must find out more about Alfred because, if we obtain a picture of the Saxons at their best from Bede, under Alfred and his immediate descendants they made a good fight before they were swamped by the Danes.

Asser the historian, who lived at the court of Alfred, tells us that he 'remained illiterate even till he was twelve years old or more; but he listened with serious attention to the Saxon poems which he often heard recited'. His father Ethelwulf sent him to Rome, in 853, and took him there again in 855. Notwithstanding the advantages of foreign travel, as late as 884 'he had not yet learned to read anything'.

When Alfred became king, he paid great attention to education. He imported Johannes Scotus from France to assist, but the schoolboys do not seem to have taken to him kindly, because we are told that he 'was pierced with the iron styles of the boys he was instructing'.

Alfred did not suffer from his own lack of schooling, because we read that he 'was affable and pleasant to all, and curiously eager to investigate things unknown'. This being the case, the king determined to acquire knowledge, and then pass it on to his subjects. He realized that History, to be of any real use to a people, must have an international flavour about it, and not be too self-consciously national; nations are like individuals and must rub shoulders.

Alfred therefore took 'The History of the World, from the Creation to 416', by Orosius, a Spaniard, and caused it to be translated into Anglo-Saxon, and while this was being done he inserted accounts of the travels of two of his contemporaries, Ohthere, and Wulfstan.

Ohthere was a Norseman, who following the adventurous habit of his people, had come to England, and had visited the Saxon Court.

Ohthere told his lord, King Alfred, that he dwelt northmost of all Northmen. [He was one of the first explorers.] He said that, at a certain time, he wished to find out how far the land lay right north; or

whether any man dwelt to the north of the waste.
Then he went right north near the land; he left, all
the way, the waste land on the right, and the wide
sea on the left, for three days. Then was he as far
north as whale-hunters ever go. He then went yet
right north, as far as he could sail in the next three
days. Then the land bent there right east, or the sea
in on the land, he knew not whether; but he knew
that he there waited for a western wind, or a little to
the north, and sailed thence east near the land, as far
as he could sail in four days. Then he must wait
there for a right north wind, because the land bent
there right south, or the sea in on the land, he knew
not whether. Then sailed he thence right south, near
the land, as far as he could sail in five days.

Ohthere had rounded the North Cape, and reached
the White Sea. He found the Biarmians living on the
shore there, and hunted horse-whales (walruses), 'because they have very good bone in their teeth . . . and
their hides are very good for ship-ropes'.

Ohthere was a wealthy man in his own country,
having 600 reindeer, 20 horned cattle, 20 sheep, and 20
swine.

Alfred's interest in sea-power and his realization of
its importance is illustrated by the well-known passage
in the Anglo-Saxon Chronicle:

Then King Alfred commanded long-ships to be
built to oppose the esks; they were full nigh twice as
long as the others; some had sixty oars, and some
had more; they were both swifter and steadier, and
also higher than the others. They were shapen
neither like the Frisian nor the Danish, but so as it
seemed to him they would be most efficient.

Unfortunately they were not very efficient vessels and were little use against the skilfully handled Viking ships.

Alfred was a great builder in other ways. He repaired London in 886. This raises a very interesting problem. Did he repair and rebuild London in the Roman manner? In Alfred's time there must have been many buildings which were nearly perfect, and he may have restored these. This is suggested by Asser, who wrote, 'What shall I say of the cities and towns which he restored . . . of the royal vills constructed of stone, removed from their old site, and handsomely rebuilt.' The Saxons would not have been able to originate a classical building, but they may have restored them. In any picture then of Saxon London, side by side with their timber halls, we must be prepared for these old Roman buildings given a new lease of life by Alfred's genius.

Asser tells how he encouraged people 'to build houses, majestic and good, beyond all the precedents of his ancestors, by his new mechanical inventions'. Whether these were wood or stone we do not know, but he built a church at Athelney on what was regarded as a new plan. He planted four posts in the ground, which formed the angles of the main structure, and around these built four aisles. This must have resembled the old Norwegian timber-framed church shown in Fig. 25, and was not at all classical, but entirely northern in conception.

A note in the Anglo-Saxon Chronicle (978) on houses suggests that the hall had been moved up to what we should now call the first floor level, where it was to remain until the fourteenth century –

In this year all the chief 'Witan' of the English

nation fell at Calne from an upper chamber, except the holy archbishop Dunstan, who alone supported himself upon a beam.

Neither houses nor churches were very comfortable. Asser tells how the king caused 6 candles to be made out of 72 pennyweights of wax; each candle had 12 divisions and lasted 4 hours, so that the 6 candles lasted through the 24 hours. But owing to the 'violence of the wind, which blew day and night without intermission through the doors and windows of the churches', the candles guttered and did not keep correct time, so the king 'ordered a lantern to be beautifully constructed of wood and white ox-horn'.

With the candles, Alfred 'so divided the twenty-four hours of the day and night as to employ eight of them in writing, in reading, and in prayer, eight in the refreshment of his body, and eight in dispatching the business of his realm'.

He had need to safeguard his time in this way, because there was so much for him to do. Laws had to be made. William of Malmesbury in the throes of extreme hero-worship, tells us how Alfred

appointed centuries, which they call 'hundreds', and decennaries, that is to say, 'tythings', so that every Englishman living, according to law, must be a member of both. If anyone was accused of a crime, he was obliged immediately to produce persons from the hundred and tything to become his surety; and whosoever was unable to find such surety, must dread the severity of the laws. If any who was impleaded made his escape either before or after he had found surety, all persons of the hundred and tything paid a fine to the king. By this regulation he diffused such peace through the country, that he ordered golden bracelets, which might mock the eager desires of the passengers while no one durst take them away, to be hung up on the public causeways, where the roads crossed each other.

The personal combat was another method of settling differences. In 1041, we read of William Malmesbury, that Gunhilda, sister of Hardicanute, and wife of Henry, Emperor of the Germans, was accused of adultery –

She opposed in single contest to her accuser, a man of gigantic size, a young lad of her brother's establishment, whom she had brought from England, while her other attendants held back in cowardly apprehension. When, therefore, they engaged, the impeacher, through the miraculous interposition of God, was worsted, by being ham-strung.

Alfred appears to have been content to concentrate the power of Wessex within its own borders, and it was left to his successors to carry war into the Danelaw. They were so successful, that under Eadred, and then Eadgar, with the assistance of Dunstan, the Danelaw submitted, and England became one kingdom; then came decline, and by the days of Aethelred the Unready, 978–1016, the whole of England passed into Danish hands. The dismal tale can be traced in the Chronicle. In that year (991) it was decreed that tribute, for the first time, should be given to the Danish men, on account of the great terror which they caused by the sea coast; that was at first 10,000 pounds. In 994 it was 16,000, and in 1002, 24,000 pounds of money.

In 1005 'was the great famine throughout the English nation; such, that no man ever before recollected one so grim'. 1009 was a tragic year. A navy had been built by a levy, 'from three hundred hides and from ten hides, one vessel; and from eight hides, a helmet and a coat of mail'. The ships were brought together at Sandwich but the whole business was wrecked by treachery and incapacity and 'they let the whole nation's toil thus lightly pass away' so that when the Danes came again they ravaged and plunderd as before, the people of East Kent paying 3000 pounds. 'Then the king commanded the whole nation to be called out; so that they should be opposed on every side: but lo! nevertheless, they marched as they pleased.'

The Chronicle contains a terrible picture of the death of Saxon Archbishop Elphege at the hands of the Danes. 'And there they then shamefully slaughtered him: they cast upon him bones and the horns of oxen, and then one of them struck him with an axe-iron on the head, so that with the blow he sank down.' But enough of Destruction. We will turn to the more pleasant task of writing of Construction, and fortunately for us, in the days between Alfred and Dunstan, there is an ample store of material on which to draw.

This will be a convenient place in which to discuss church build- ings. Fig. 34 is the plan, and Fig. 35 the in- terior of Wing Church, Buck- inghamshire. On page 56 it will be seen that the Christian

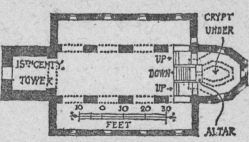

Fig. 34 Plan of Wing Church, Buckinghamshire

Fig. 35 The interior of Wing Church (partial reconstruction)

Fig. 36   East end of Wing Church (partial reconstruction)

Church which was built at Silchester was called
basilican, because it resembled the Basilica, or Hall
of Justice, there. This Roman tradition of building
was adopted at Wing, but the apse is polygonal, instead of being semi-circular as at Silchester. We think
it is later than the nave, and Fig. 36 shows how the
exterior has the narrow strips of stone, which are
characteristic of some Saxon buildings. The apse covers
the crypt, or confessio, where a saintly man was buried,

and this was so arranged that it could be seen into from the nave, and from openings on the outside. These crypts developed from the practice of worshipping in the catacombs at Rome at the graves of the early martyrs.

Fig. 38 shows a window opening at Wing, with the curious mid-wall shaft, which was the forerunner of

Fig. 37   Worth, Sussex

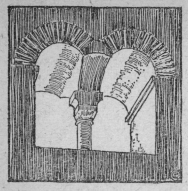

Fig. 38 A window at Wing Church

the traceried window. The next step is shown in Fig. 64.

Fig. 37, of Worth Church, Sussex, shows another Saxon church of basilican type, with an apsidal east end. In the typical basilica, the bishop's chair stood in the centre of the apse, and the clergy sat on a bench around the wall. The altar stood on the chord of the apse. The choir was in front of the altar, with the catechumens, or those who were being instructed, in the nave. The women sat in one aisle, the men in the other, and the penitents in the porch.

Figs. 41, 43, of the Saxon church at Bradford-on-Avon, Wiltshire, show the type of plan with a square ended chancel, which was to become the more usual English type of church. This church is one of the earliest churches known in the south of England. It was founded by Aldhelm at the end of the seventh century and was later reconstructed in the tenth century.

When the Saxons first began to build in stone, they imitated many of the details of timber buildings.

Fig. 39 Worth: Nave windows

Fig. 40   Sculpture at Bradford-on-Avon Church

This is very apparent in the tower at Earls Barton, Northamptonshire (Fig. 42). Great care was taken here to cut back the masonry, so that only the narrow strips of stone were visible and the walls between were plastered. The angle quoins, built with alternate long and short stones, are another typical Saxon detail. The

Fig. 41   Interior of
Bradford-on-Avon Church

towers of Saxon churches appear to have been used to house the sacristans on the first floor, to which access was gained by a wooden ladder. There were openings in the east wall of the tower which enabled the sacristan to keep watch over the church.

In the basilican churches the porch, or narthex, at first extended right across the width of the church. Later it was abbreviated into a western porch and this was then raised into a tower. Fig. 44

Fig. 42 Tower of Earls Barton Church, Northamptonshire
(partial reconstruction)

Fig. 43 (*above*)   Exterior of Bradford-on-Avon Church, Wiltshire

Fig. 44   Tower doorway, Earls
Barton Church

Fig. 45   St. Benet's Church,
Cambridge: tower arch

Sompting. Sussex
Tower arch
June '25. CHB.

Fig. 46   Tower arch, Sompting Church, Sussex

Fig. 47   Tower of Sompting Church

shows the tower doorway at Earls Barton, and how one of the stone strips was curved around it. Fig. 45, of the tower arch at St. Benet's Church, Cambridge, from the nave, shows this same detail on a larger scale, as well as the opening over it from which the sacristan could look down into the church from his room in the tower.

Fig 46 shows the very fine tower arch at Sompting, Sussex, and Fig. 47, of the exterior, is interesting as it is the only Saxon tower in England which has its original form of roof.

The ordinary churches were timber built. Edwin was baptized at York in 627

> in the Church of St. Peter the Apostle, which he himself had built of timber ... but as soon as he was baptized, he took care by the direction of the same Paulinus, to build in the same place a larger and nobler church of stone in the midst whereof that same oratory which he had first erected should be enclosed.

Fig. 48   Head of Tau. Crozier of walrus ivory, found at Alcester, Warwickshire. Early eleventh century (*British Museum*)

So the wooden oratory was the fore-runner of the present cathedral.

Bells were used in churches. Bede tells how a nun on the night of St. Hilda's death, 'on a sudden heard the well-known sound of a bell in the air, which used to awake and call them to prayers'.

The British Museum possesses an interesting relic in the iron bell of St. Cuilleann, which was enshrined in bronze in the eleventh century. Evidently the early saints used ordinary cow-bells to summon their people, and these later became sacred relics. Their walking-sticks were treasured, and cased in metal became the type for the pastoral staff of a bishop.

Lack of space prevents us from dealing more fully with church architecture. The sketches we have given are sufficient to show that the art of the Saxon builder was sturdy and vigorous, and as the greater part of it is found in the Eastern and Midland counties, some of the credit must be given to the Danes and Vikings who settled in these parts. It should be remembered that we have to judge the builders by their smaller churches; the larger cathedrals were pulled down and rebuilt by the Normans.

Christianity meant the introduction of a new set of symbols into the world; these were very necessary when many people could not read. Heraldry was a form of symbolism, and also the later tradesmen's signs. The Church used the fish as a symbol of the Saviour, because the initials of the Greek words for 'Jesus Christ, Son of God, Saviour' form the Greek word for fish. The Church was shown as a ship in which the faithful sailed safely across the sea of life, and Hope was typified as an anchor. Christ was the Good Shepherd, and the Devil a serpent. The soul of the

Fig. 49   St. Mark

Fig. 50   St. Matthew

Fig. 51   St. Luke

Fig. 52   St. Mark

Fig. 53   St. Mark

Fig. 54   St. John

SYMBOLS OF THE EVANGELISTS
(Figs. 49–52, 54 from the Gospels of St. Chad; Fig. 53 from the Gospels of Durrow)

departed was shown as a dove, and Victory as a palm branch; Immortality by a peacock; the Resurrection by the phoenix, and the soul thirsting for baptism as a stag. The triangle was the Trinity. The sacred monogram, or Chi-Rho, was formed of the first two letters of the Greek word for Christ. The Cross itself was used as a symbol in varying forms. The Tau (Fig. 48), from the Greek character T; the St. Andrew's Cross like the Latin numeral X; the Latin Cross with the longer lower limb. The Evangelists each had their symbols: the Angel for St. Matthew, the Lion for St. Mark, the Ox for St. Luke and the Eagle for St. John (Figs. 49–54).

Monasticism was introduced into this country in Saxon times. The practice was first begun by the anchorites, who in Egypt, in the third century, withdrew to the desert to pass their life in solitude and devotion. St. Pachomius organized them into a community at Tabennisi, near Denderah, 315–20, and this led to the Coptic and Abyssinian churches. The next development was in Syria, early in the fourth century, and, in the latter half, St. Basil, of Caesarea, instituted a system in Cappadocia. About 500, St. Benedict founded the great system, which bears his name, at the monastery of Monte Cassino, between Rome and Naples, which was to exercise so enormous an influence. Here in England, in Saxon times, the Rule was not followed with great strictness. In the Irish monasteries the monks, when at home, lived in separate cells, and when abroad preached the Gospel as missionaries. In the Benedictine monastery, the monks lived, prayed, and slept together in common. They were celebrated for their learning, and built fine churches; they cultivated the waste lands and were good farmers; they gave shelter to the scholar and the artist, and in a rough and turbulent age the cloak of religion was a better protection than the sword.

Here is the rent which the Abbot of Medeshamstede (Peterborough) charged for land that he let to Wilfrid,

> each year should deliver into the minster sixty loads of wood, and twelve of coal and six of faggots, and two tuns full of pure ale, and two beasts fit for slaughter, and six hundred loaves, and ten measures of Welsh ale, and each year a horse and thirty shillings, and one day's entertainment.

This is an interesting passage because it shows that, though the usual method of trade was to barter commodities, yet money was in use as a means of exchange.

The Sceatta currency, and the Northumbrian styca, came before the penny first struck by Offa of Mercia. Many hoards of Anglo-Saxon coins have been discovered in this country, the most important being the find made in 1840, in a leaden chest near a ford over the Ribble, above Preston. It contained 10,000 silver coins, and nearly 1000 ozs of silver; it was buried between 903 and 905 and may have been the treasure chest of a Danish army. Coins have been found at Rome of Offa, 757–96, and may have been 'Peter's Pence'. Many more Anglo-Saxon coins have been found in Sweden than have been found in England. These Scandinavian finds presumably represent part of the Dane-geld – the tax paid by the English to buy off the Viking raiders. At the same time the presence of these coins in Scandinavia is a tribute to the high standard of the English coinage, for at this time the coinage of England was superior in quality and uniformity to any in Europe.

Church dues were a very heavy charge on industry in these early days. Canute wrote to Ethelnoth, to take care that

> all dues owing to ancient custom be discharged: that is to say, plough-alms (a penny to the poor for as much land as a plough could till), the tenth of animals born in the current year, and the pence owing to Rome for St. Peter; and in the middle of August the tenth of the produce of the earth; and on the festival of St. Martin, the first fruits of the seeds (a sack of corn from every load), to the church and the parish where each one resides.

People complain of high taxation in these days, but here was an Income Tax, not on the profit of the year, but the whole turn-over.

The Church gave very good value for the money received, because not only were the souls of the people saved, but their everyday life was regulated. Dunstan observed that

> as his countrymen used to assemble in taverns, and when a little elevated quarrel as to the proportion of their liquor, he ordered gold or silver pegs to be fastened in the pots, that whilst every man knew his just measure, shame should compel each neither to take more himself nor oblige others to drink beyond their proportional share.

The Church at an early date encouraged pilgrimage. We read in the Chronicle (816): 'The same year the English School at Rome was burned.' This was near St. Peter's, for the accommodation of pilgrims. These pilgrimages played their part in educating and interesting people, and as the Church of Rome has always been very democratic, the son of a peasant could become first priest, then prelate, and, going to Rome, come back and tell his friends of all the fine things he had seen there. It is interesting to note, however, that many Anglo-Saxon craftsmen lived in Rome and that Anglo-Saxon metalworkers, working in Rome, supplied some of the sacred vessels for St. Peter's itself.

Aelfric is another of the churchmen who have left us a picture of Saxon times. He was a monk in the New Minster (Winchester), founded in the time of Eadgar (958–75). He tells of the ranks into which the people were divided, and it is evident that by his time there was less freedom than there had been. We have seen how in Alfred's time it became necessary to put the safety of the State before the comfort of the people. Formerly the main division was between 'eorles' and 'ceorles', or gentle and simple, but if the 'ceorl' thrived and had five hides of land, a church, kitchen, and a place in the king's hall, then he became worthy of Thane-right, and so could the merchant and the thane become an 'eorl'.

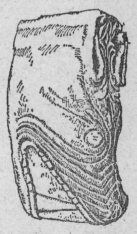

Aelfric, in his 'Colloquies', tells us of the duties of men, and these by the time of Canute had been so regulated, that every man had his job and definite position in the State. The thegn held his land on condition that he rendered military service, and undertook the repair of fortifications, and bridge building. The geneat, cottar, and

Fig. 55 Carving at Deerhurst Church, Gloucestershire

gebur were retainers, or tenants, of the thegn, or lord, and held their land on condition that they supported him. The beekeeper, swineherd, oxherd, cowherd, shepherd, goatherd, cheesemaker, barnman, beadle, woodward, hayward, and the sowers all had their dues and duties defined. The keepers of animals had to guard them as well. Edgar 'commanded Judwall, king of the Welsh, to pay him yearly a tribute of three hundred

Fig. 56 Funeral of Edward the Confessor (Bayeux tapestry)

wolves'. The slaves were not forgotten. A slave woman was entitled to eight pounds of corn for food, one sheep or three pennies for winter food, one sester of beans for Lenten fare, and in summer whey, or one penny. As well they were entitled to a feast at Christmas, and another at Easter, and a handful of corn at harvest beside their other dues. We do not know if Canute himself laid down these rules. In them it is stated that though customs varied, those mentioned were the general ones, yet if better could be found they would be gladly approved.

In viewing these customs ourselves we must not condemn them too hastily as having been based on slavery. The system was very closely knit and strong because it was based on the land. Our own world, for

little more than a century (which, historically speak-
ing, is only a flicker of time) has toyed with the ideas
of freedom and liberty, and an industrial system which
is weak because it is divorced from the land. Today
whole classes of people are dependent on others for
their schooling and books; have to be assisted to build
houses, and have baths, and receive doles when they
are unemployed, and subsidies when trade is bad. And
we import nearly all our food. If Canute could have
contrasted our customs with his own he might not have
been greatly chagrined.

Perhaps the final note in this part should be one on
the spread of knowledge which made possible the
developments of the next period. William of Malmesbury tells of the training of Pope Silvester (1002), who
travelled among the Saracens in the South of Spain.
He practised the use of the astrolabe for making
celestial observations, became skilled in astronomy and
astrology; he acquired the art of calling up spirits from
hell – arithmetic, music, and geometry; learned to use
the abacus or counting table. Later in Gaul, when
Archbishop of Rheims, he constructed a clock on
'mechanical principles, and an hydraulic organ, in
which the air, escaping in a surprising manner, by the
force of heated water, fills the cavity of the instrument,
and the brazen pipes emit modulated tones through the
multifarious apertures'.

3

THE COMING OF THE NORMANS

IN this chapter we arrive at the period with which we start in Volume I of *A History of Everyday Things in England*. In that book we deal with the appearance of the Norman people and their ships, castles, monasteries cathedrals, games, and general customs. We shall not, therefore, cover the same ground again, but seek for new types so that the two books may be complementary one to the other.

We think that the more the Normans are studied the greater respect one has for their energy and intelligence, but it needs some explanation why so much became possible to them. They were of the same Nordic type as the Saxons and Vikings, and it was as the Northmen, or Norsemen, that they settled in Normandy, under Hrolf, in 912, and, as we showed on page 79, very unpleasant neighbours the French found them.

We will now try to find out what kind of people they were. Our principal authority will be Master Wace and his Chronicle of the Norman Conquest from the Roman de Rou. Wace was a trouvère or troubadour at the court of Henry II, and his sprightly tale forms an admirable text to the pictures of the tapestry at Bayeux, which is another great record of the Conquest.

Wace gives us a graphic picture of life in Normandy when William was forging the sword with which to conquer England. His barons were turbulent, and before they could be welded into a whole by feudalism had to be persuaded to leave off killing one another. The Truce of God was introduced by William, in 1061, and enforced by him as a restraint on the Normans.

He made all swear on the relics to hold peace and maintain it from sunset on Wednesday to sunrise on Monday. This was called the TRUCE, and the like of it I believe is not in any country. If any man should beat another meantime, or do him any mischief, or any of his goods, he was to be excommunicated, and amerced nine livres to the bishop.

Harold, on his way to Normandy, was taken prisoner by the Count of Ponthieu, and delivered up to William, who thus appeared to come to Harold's rescue. He was nobly entertained by the duke, and then trapped into promising to deliver England to the Norman on the death of Edward. To receive the oath, William caused a Parliament to be called. As well,

Fig. 57   The building of William's fleet (Bayeux tapestry)

Fig. 58 A carpenter   *Fig. 59* William's sappers

He sent for all the holy bodies thither, and put so many of them together as to fill a whole chest, and then covered them with a pall; but Harold neither saw them, nor knew of them being there; for nought was shown or told to him about it; and over all was a phylactery, the best that he could select; oeil de boeuf, I have heard it called. When Harold placed his hand upon it, the hand trembled and the flesh quivered; but he swore and promised upon his oath to take Ele to wife, and to deliver up England to the duke . . . when Harold . . . had risen upon his feet, the duke led him up to the chest, and made him stand near it; and took off the chest the pall that had covered it, and shewed Harold upon what holy relics he had sworn, and he was sorely alarmed at the sight.

We can read in Wace how, when Harold failed to keep his promise, the preparations for the conquest went forward. William received gifts and promises of men and ships; the old Viking spirit of adventure came into play again, and the signs were auspicious.

Now while these things were doing, a great star

appeared, shining for fourteen days, with three long rays streaming towards the south; such a star as is wont to be seen when a kingdom is about to change its king. [There was great enthusiasm]. William got together carpenters, smiths, and other workmen, so that great stir was seen at all the ports of Normandy, in the collecting of wood and materials, cutting of planks, framing of ships and boats, stretching sails and rearing masts, with great pains and at great cost. They spent all one summer and autumn in fitting up the fleet and collecting the forces.

Then the time came when they were ready to sail, and

they prayed the convent to bring out the shrine of S. Valeri, and set it on a carpet in the plain; and all came praying the holy reliques, that they might be allowed to pass over sea. They offered so much money, that the reliques were buried beneath it; and from that day forth, they had good weather and a fair wind.

Wace tells how

I heard my father say – I remember it well, although I was but a lad – that there were seven hundred ships, less four, when they sailed from S. Valeri; and that there were besides these ships, boats and skiffs for the purpose of carrying the arms and harness. [And when at length they started] The Duke placed a lantern on the mast of his ship that the other ships might see it, and hold their course after it.

Fig. 60.   William's army cooks

When they reached England,

As the ships were drawn to shore, and the Duke first landed, he fell by chance upon his two hands. Forthwith all raised a loud cry of distress, 'an evil sign,' said they, 'is here.' But he cried out lustily, 'See, seignors, by the splendour of God! I have seized England with my two hands; without challenge no prize can be made; all is our own that is here; and now we shall see who is the bolder man.'

The archers

touched the land foremost, each with his bow bent and his quiver full of arrows slung at his side. All were shaven and shorn, and all clad in short garments, ready to attack, to shoot, to wheel about and skirmish. The knights landed next, all armed; with their hauberks on, their shields slung at their necks, and their helmets laced. They formed together on the shore, each armed upon his warhorse. All had their swords girded on, and passed into the plain with their lances raised. The barons had gonfanons, and the

Fig. 61   William's army cooks

knights pennons. They occupied the advanced
ground, next to where the archers had fixed themselves. The carpenters, who came after, had great
axes in the hands, and planes and adzes at their sides.
When they had reached the spot where the archers
stood, and the knights were assembled, they consulted together, and sought for a good spot to place
a strong fort upon. Then they cast out of the ships
the materials and drew them to land, all shaped,
framed and pierced to receive the pins which they
had brought, cut and ready in large barrels; so that
before evening had well set in, they had finished a
fort. [Later a knight describes how] he saw them
build up and enclose a fort, and dig the fosse around
it [and] they strengthened it round about with
palisades and a fosse.

The castle which Wace describes is similar to that
shown on the Bayeux tapestry, which we illustrate in
Fig. 62. It is called now the motte-and-bailey type.
The motte was formed by scarping down a natural hill,
or raising an artificial one with the earth dug out of the
ditches. On this the fort was built and surrounded by a
timber palisade. The ditch of the motte also encircled
the bailey, and here were the stables, barns, kitchens,
and barracks. The site always included a good spring
of water. In such a castle William could leave a garrison
to hold down the countryside. The Saxons had nothing
so scientific at their disposal. Just as the Viking, with
his ship as a base and his horse to carry him about,
could deliver a blow at his own time, so the Normans,
in the security of their castles, could select the moment
for attack.

William knew all about building stone castles. Wace
tells us how William of Arques built a tower above

Fig. 62   Motte-and-Bailey Castle

Arches (Chateau d'Arques, near Dieppe), and was
besieged there by Duke William. The King of France
came to the assistance of William of Arques, and Duke
William, hearing of his intention, 'strengthened his
castles, cleaning the fosses, and repairing the walls. . . .
Caen was then without a castle, and had neither wall
nor fence to protect it.' Stone walls are evidently meant
here and differentiated from wooden fences or palisades. William built timber castles at first in England
because they could be constructed quickly.

We can now return to the details of the Conquest
and as the pages of Wace are read one becomes very
sorry for the Saxons; they were beaten by the most
wonderful staff work. William not only brought over
castles packed in casks, but remembered that armies
march on their stomachs. Wace tells how

> you might see them make their kitchens, light their
> fires, and cook their meat. The duke sat down to eat,
> and the barons and knights had food in plenty; for he
> had brought ample store. All ate and drank enough,
> and were right glad that they were ashore.

The Bayeux tapestry shows the Normans arriving
at Pevensey, but according to Wace they first landed
near Hastings and William 'ordered proclamation to
be made, and commanded the sailors that the ships
should be dismantled, and drawn ashore and pierced,
that the cowards might not have the ships to flee to'.
This can only be regarded as a gesture to his men that
they must do or die. William would hardly have cut off
his line of retreat, or have built a fort at Hastings,
except to leave a garrison in it to safeguard the fleet.

T—E

His next step was to move west about 12 miles to Pevensey. 'The English were to be seen fleeing before them, driving off their cattle, and quitting their houses. All took shelter in the cemeteries, and even there they were in grievous alarm.' Here again is evidence of staff work. Pevensey was one of the forts built about AD 300 by the Romans to protect the east and south coasts from the Saxon raids. As the Roman walls with their bastions enclosing several acres are still standing today, they must, in William's time, have formed a good strong base where he could be safe and so compel Harold to come to him.

This was what poor Harold had to do. He came post haste from the Humber, from his encounter with Tosti, first to London, and then south again, and 'erected his standard and fixed his gonfalon right where the Abbey of the Battle is now built', about 9 miles away from William at Pevensey. Here Harold dug himself in. 'He had the place well examined and surrounded it by a good fosse, leaving an entrance on each of the three sides, which were ordered to be all well guarded.'

We shall not concern ourselves very much with the details of the fighting, but there is one very interesting detail which must be noted. In the old Viking days, and the tale of Burnt Njal, fighting is mentioned quite casually, as fishing might be, or hunting. It was undertaken as a sport. From the time of the Normans onwards people sought to justify themselves. There were many parleys in 1066, and much talk of the justice of the respective causes. Each side appealed for the favour of Heaven, and there were threats of the dire consequences which would befall the opponent. The combatants, like modern boxers, reassured themselves and their backers, and appear to have stood in need of support. When William prepared to arm himself, he called first for his good hauberk, and a man brought it on his arm and placed it before him; but in putting his head in to get it on, he inadvertently turned it the wrong way, with the back part in front. He quickly changed it, but when he saw that those who stood by were sorely alarmed, he said, 'I have seen many a man who, if such a thing happened to him, would not have borne arms or entered the field the same day; but I never believed in omens, and I never will. I trust in God.'

One of Harold's spies, who had seen the Normans, reported that they 'were so close shaven and cropt, that they had not even moustaches, supposed he had seen priests and mass-sayers; and he told Harold that the duke had more priests with him than knights or other people'. But Harold replied, 'Those are valiant knights, bold and brave warriors, though they bear not beards or moustaches as we do.' William's priests were quite prepared to be useful. 'Odo, the good priest, the bishop of Bayeux, "was always found" where the battle was most fierce, and was of great service on that day.'

After the battle, 'The English who escaped from the field did not stop till they reached London.' Again there is evidence of wonderful staff work. William did not at once pursue the enemy, but turned his attention to consolidating his position.

If our readers refer to the map of Roman Britain published by the Ordnance Survey, it will be seen why William selected Hastings as his point of attack. Pevensey was close by, all by itself and so more vulnerable. On the other hand, the usual entrance into England, by Watling Street, was protected by a group of forts at Lympne, Folkestone, Dover, Richborough, and Reculver. Some of these must have been in repair, because we read in Wace of how William went back east to Romney, which he destroyed, and then on to Dover. Obviously some Norman troops had been detailed to hold the English in check, and prevent them coming to the assistance of Harold, because Wace says that William did not rest 'till he reached Dover, at the strong fort he had ordered to be made at the foot of the hill'. Here he besieged the old Roman fort, and though the place was well fortified, took it after an eight-day siege. William placed a garrison in it, and was now ready for the great adventure; he had won a great battle; could he hold the country?

Canterbury rendered homage and delivered hostages to the Conqueror, who then journeyed to London. Arrived at Southwark, the citizens issued out of the gates, but were speedily driven back, and the Normans burned all the houses on the south side of the Thames Here again William gave another proof of genius. He had given the Londoners a taste of his quality, and his most urgent need was to thrust a spearhead in between his enemies before they had the opportunity to gather their forces together. This William did by going to Wallingford on the Thames, where it is thought that he crossed, and then passed by Icknield Way to the gap in the Chilterns at Tring, and then on to Berkhamsted. Again we will look at the map of Roman Britain and note that William's last raid gave him possession of many of the roads leading into London. First there was Stane Street from Portsmouth and Chichester. Then the very important road crossing the Thames at Staines, which branched off at Silchester into three roads serving the south and west. At Tring, William cut across Akeman Street, and could control Watling Street at Dunstable. The strategy was brilliantly successful, because the English surrendered and William received the crown of England in the grounds of Berkhamsted Castle.

We can now pass on to the work of the Normans when they were established in the country, and Fig. 63 shows a reconstruction of Berkhamsted Castle. It is supposed that the earthworks and the mount are the work of Robert, Count of Mortain, who was in possession of Berkhamsted at the time of Domesday. Little remains now except earthworks and broken walls to mark an historic site, one which has seen perhaps as much of both the gay and the busy side of medieval life as any of our more ancient castles except Windsor. Thomas Becket was in charge of the works from 1155 to 1165. Edward III and the Black Prince held their courts within its walls. Froissart was another inhabitant, and Geoffrey Chaucer another clerk of the works. In 1930 this sadly neglected relic was placed under the guardianship of the Ministry of Works and put into a state of preservation.

The plan is of great interest because it shows the development of what is called the shell keep. As the artificial mottes became consolidated, the timber forts (Fig. 62) were replaced with a stone wall. At Berkhamsted (Fig. 63), when the mottes was excavated, it was discovered that this shell was about 60 feet external diameter, the wall being 8 feet thick. There would have been a rampart walk on the top of this, and various sheds around it inside. There were steps up the motte, and these were protected by a tower at the top, and by the moat or ditch being taken around the motte at the base. The bailey had an inner and outer ward, and these were surrounded by flint rubble walls about 7 feet thick, of which some few parts remain. These had bastions and gates as shown, and were further protected by the two ditches and bank between, which make the castle so interesting.

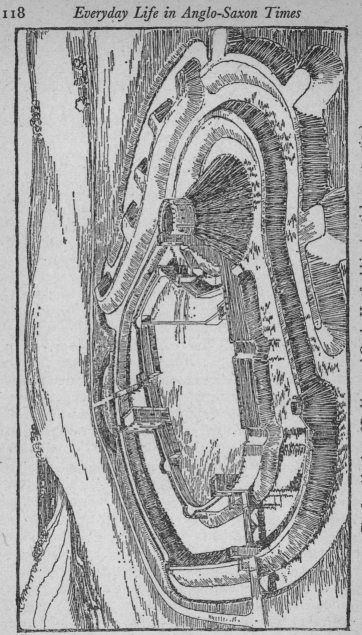

Fig. 63 Air view of Berkhamsted Castle, Hertfordshire (partial reconstruction)

The next development of the castle is shown in Volume I of *Everyday Things in England*.

We will now describe one of the most interesting buildings in England, the Norman House at Christchurch, Hampshire, the ruins of which are situated in the garden of the King's Head Hotel. The important detail to remember is that the English house started its life as a hall. On page 30 we have given a description of the hall in Beowulf, but here at Christchurch we can leave literary evidence behind, and look at the actual stones of an early twelfth-century house. It started life as the hall of the castle, and was built between 1125 and 1150. In Beowulf the hall is obviously on the ground floor level, but at Christchurch it has been moved to the first floor. This gave more sense of security, and enabled the windows to be bigger than would have been possible on the level of the ground. These had no glass, only wooden shutters for use at night. The hall was to remain on the first floor until life became a little more secure, in the fourteenth century, when it was moved downstairs, as at Penshurst.

Unfortunately the very considerable remains at Christchurch are so swathed with ivy that the walls are not only being destroyed, but it is very difficult to form any idea of what the building used to look like. However we have made a careful survey of the ruins, and Figs. 64 and 65 are our reconstructions. The plan is very simple, just one large hall on the first floor, where the family lived, ate, and slept, because there was nowhere else to go. One remarkable detail is that there is a good fireplace in the hall, yet, side by side, the old custom of the fire in the centre of the hall was to remain till as late as 1570 at the Middle Temple Hall.

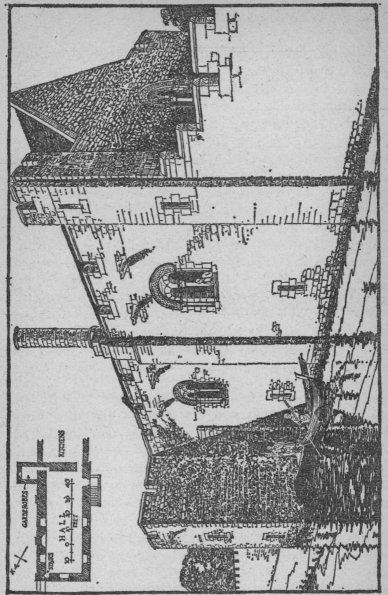

Fig. 64   Exterior of the Norman house at Christchurch, Hampshire (partial reconstruction)

Fig. 65 The hall of the Norman house at Christchurch (partial reconstruction)

At Christchurch the kitchens came at the south end of the hall, where also were the garderobes or latrines. At the north end was a circular staircase, which led up to the ramparts and down to a large room on the level of the ground, where doubtless men-at-arms and stores were. Then, of course, there would have been many sheds, stables, and barns, in the castle bailey, which was surrounded by a wall. The house was built as part of this wall, so that the inhabitants could look across the mill stream, to which access was gained by a water gate (Fig. 64). The development of the house plan is

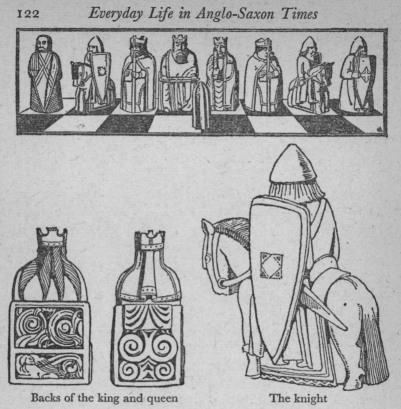

Backs of the king and queen　　　　　The knight

Figs. 66–9　Chessmen found at Uig, Isle of Lewis, carved in morse ivory.
Twelfth century (*British Museum*)

shown in Volume I of *Everyday Things in England*, where
it can be seen how other rooms were gradually grouped
around the hall, until, in the fifteenth century, the hall
had become a house as we understand it.

Figs. 66–9 are of a magnificent set of chessmen now
in the British Museum. They are carved in morse ivory
and were found at Uig in the Isle of Lewis. They date
from the twelfth century. The people in the hall at
Christchurch may have played chess with chessmen
like these. The king stands 4 inches high. The warders,

one biting his shield in rage, which take the place of the castles, should be noted.

Now we are approaching the end of our task, and with superb artistry have kept the really triumphant achievement of the Normans for our finale! Unless we are careful, we look back and think only of their castles; we may have been to the Tower of London, or have caught sight of Rochester on our way along that very old way, Watling Street, or we may have been to Castle Hedingham, Essex. These three wonderful keeps may have oppressed our spirits, as they did the Saxons who were held in thrall under their walls. Stare, stark, and strong, these great walls rear themselves up, yet they are full of delightful little bits of detail which gladden the architect. Judged only by their castles, the Normans would seem too fierce and formidable, but when we come to their cathedrals and churches, there is a very different tale to tell. The architecture is still fierce and proud. It lacks the grace of the thirteenth century, and makes you think of a race of priests who could challenge kings and usurers. Abbot Samson, of whom Carlyle wrote in *Past and Present*, and Becket were of the same breed – turbulent, but very strong, and not given to compromise or half measures in their fight against evil. There is hardly a cathedral in England in which their hand cannot be traced, and their vision and grasp of planning was superb; it was almost as if they took William's favourite oath as their motto and built to the 'Splendour of God'. The zenith of the architectural achievement of the Normans can be seen at Durham, where the great Norman cathedral is one of the most impressive churches of its period in Western Europe.

We have selected for our illustrations, not a

Fig. 70   The interior of Hemel Hempstead Church, Hertfordshire
(partial reconstruction)

cathedral, but the church of Hemel Hempstead, Hertfordshire, which shows how the Normans went to work when they wanted to build a parish church in a small market town about 1140.

The plan (Fig. 72) shows that the men of Hemel Hempstead, in 1140, understood the value of a simple layout of cruciform type, and fig. 70 how this resolved itself into a wonderful interior, in which one looked through darkness into light. Fig. 71 is the exterior. Our illustrations have been made from sketches of the actual building, and the few liberties we have taken have only been in the way of eliminating later work and restoring the Norman detail: internally, we have omitted the modern 'Gothic' choir stalls, and externally the later leaded spire is not shown on the Norman tower, and so on. The church has, fortunately for us, escaped the vandalism of the nineteenth century in a surprising fashion.

Fig. 73 shows the vaulting to the chancel, and is an amusing example of how the old masons played with the problems of solid geometry. The Normans at first used the plain semi-circular barrel vault. Then one day somebody made two of these vaults cross as A (Fig. 73), but the result did not satisfy them for long, because the intersections, or groins, at B, were necessarily flatter than a semi-circle; they had to be, because their span was greater than that of the vault, and they had to spring, and finish, at the same levels. So the next step was to make the groin itself semi-circular, as shown in the main drawing of fig. 73 at C. Then the cross ribs at D had to be raised up on legs, or stilted, to reach to the height of the groins. This was really a little clumsy, so the cross rib was turned into a pointed arch. But that is another story which is told in Volume I of *Everyday Things in England*, where we

Fig. 71   Exterior of Hemel Hempstead Church (partial reconstruction)

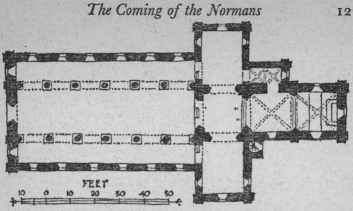

Fig. 72   Plan of Hemel Hempstead Church

show how step by step the old masons progressed up
to the glorious fan vaulting of Henry the VII's
Chapel at Westminster Abbey.

If this church at Hemel Hempstead is compared
with those of the Anglo-Saxons we have illustrated, it
will be noted how great an advance the Normans
made in the art of building; there is no fumbling with
their work, but a splendid self-confidence. They were
a wonderful people and
their stock first comes into
notice with the Norsemen,
or Northmen, who raided
our land as Vikings. We
must bear in mind their
travels to the East through
Russia, their discoveries
by land, and their adven-
tures by sea. They were a
people, and it is a period,
to which far more detailed
study should be given
than is possible in this
little book.

Fig. 73
Chancel vaulting,
Hemel Hempstead Church

England has welcomed many men. The man of the Old Stone Age; the Mediterranean men of the New Stone Age; and the Celts. Rome and her legionaries brought blood from all over Europe. Then came the Angles, Saxons, and Jutes; the Vikings and Normans; the Angevins, Flemings, Huguenots, and all the other races who have drifted in. Age after age the soil of our island has attracted men; here they have lived and, dying, their bones or ashes have been turned into the soil of England. Each in their turn have made their contribution to the common stock, and the genius of the race, and the Viking, Norseman, or Norman, was not the least of these men. It may well be that England will go forward just so long as their courage and love of adventure are not allowed to be swamped by the vulgar chaffering of the market place.

CHRONOLOGY

THE ROMAN OCCUPATION OF BRITAIN

BC

55   CAESAR makes a reconnaissance and returns to Gaul.

54   CAESAR invades in force: marches into Kent, defeats CASSIVELLAUNUS, and once more retires to Gaul.
     CAESAR's attempt to conquer Britain has failed. Celtic chieftains again hold undisputed sway.

AD

43   CLAUDIUS invades. His expeditionary force, under AULUS PLAUTIUS, lands at Richborough. CARACTACUS and TOGODUMNUS are defeated on the Medway. Verulam becomes a *municipium*. CLAUDIUS occupies Colchester. The legions push slowly northwards and westwards, the future Emperor VESPASIAN commanding the Second Legion.

47   P. OSTORIUS SCAPULA succeeds PLAUTIUS as Governor. He creates a frontier on the Fosse Way. He moves against CARACTACUS, now military leader of the Silures of South Wales.

51   OSTORIUS defeats CARACTACUS, who flees to CARTIMANDUA, Queen of the Brigantes, and is betrayed by her to the Romans. He ends his days as a prisoner at Rome.

53   The Silures fight on. OSTORIUS dies, worn out by his exertions, and is succeeded by the unenterprising DIDIUS GALLUS.

58   The enterprising D. VERANIUS NEPOS sets out to cow the Silures, but dies within the year.

59   C. SUETONIUS PAULINUS, an able and ruthless general, becomes Governor and marches into Wales.

61   PAULINUS reaches the Menai Straits. He invades Anglesey, last refuge of the Druids, and puts them to the sword. But BOUDICCA (BOADICEA), Queen of the Iceni, has revolted in far-off Norfolk. While PAULINUS

races back with his cavalry, she sacks Colchester and
annihilates the Ninth Legion. Then she destroys Verulam
and London, nearly succeeding in driving the Romans from
Britain. PAULINUS wins a brilliant victory against
superior numbers. BOUDICCA takes poison. Reprisals of
the utmost severity follow the revolt. The Procurator,
JULIUS CLASSICIANUS, protests against PAULINUS'
inhumanity. The Emperor NERO replaces PAULINUS by
C. PETRONIUS TURPILIANUS.

63　TREBELLIUS MAXIMUS becomes Governor. Compara-
tive peace in Britain.

71　The Brigantes become restless. The harsh PETILLIUS
CERIALIS is sent by VESPASIAN to subdue them.

74　The determined SEXTUS JULIUS FRONTINUS is made
Governor. He succeeds in the task of suppressing the Welsh
tribes.

78　GNAEUS JULIUS AGRICOLA, third of VESPASIAN's
fighting Governors, extinguishes the last sparks of Welsh
and Brigantian resistance.

81　AGRICOLA makes himself master of Scotland, as far as the
Forth and Clyde.

83　AGRICOLA thrusts into the Highlands and beats the
massed Caledonian armies at Mons Graupius, a celebrated
encounter.

84　The Emperor DOMITIAN, preoccupied with his German
campaigns, recalls AGRICOLA at the victorious climax of
his Governorship, AGRICOLA leaves Britain an embit-
tered man.

　　Records are scanty for British military history in the latter
part of the reign of DOMITIAN and in the reign of
TRAJAN. Names of Governors preserved in inscriptions
are:

SALLUSTIUS LUCULLUS.
NEPOS.

98　T. AVIDIUS QUIETUS.

103　L. NERIATUS MARCELLUS.
Reign of HADRIAN begins.
Q. POMPEIUS FALCO.

121　The Emperor HADRIAN visits Britain.

122　A. PLATORIUS NEPOS, an intimate friend of the Emperor, constructs Hadrian's Wall between 122–126–7.

130 JULIUS SEVERUS becomes Governor.

140 Q. LOLLIUS URBICUS, the next Governor, campaigns in Scotland. He builds the Antonine Wall, of turf, across the Forth–Clyde isthmus between 140–142–3.

155 The Brigantes revolt and are put down by C. JULIUS VERUS.

169 The Emperor MARCUS AURELIUS sends reinforcements to M. STATIUS PRISCUS, who has succeeded VERUS. Britain is again fanned by the flame of revolt.

180 At the beginning of the reign of the Emperor COMMODUS, the Caledonians burst through the Antonine Wall. It is at this point that the military initiative in Britain passes from the Romans to their enemies, with whom it remains to the end of the occupation.

184 The war in Britain ends. COMMODUS assumes the title BRITANNICUS to commemorate the victory, due to the efforts of the stern ULPIUS MARCELLUS.

185 HELVIUS PERTINAX succeeds MARCELLUS and puts down a mutiny in the Roman army in Britain.

193 COMMODUS is assassinated. The Praetorian Guard elects PERTINAX Emperor, then turns on him and butchers him. There is civil war in Rome. SEPTIMIUS SEVERUS seizes power. CLODIUS ALBINUS, successor of PERTINAX in Britain, proclaims himself Emperor and crosses with his troops to Gaul.

196 SEVERUS marches on Lyons, where ALBINUS has set up court. ALBINUS commits suicide. In consequence of the removal of the garrison by ALBINUS in his bid for the throne, the Barbarians overrun all N. England, wrecking Hadrian's Wall and dismantling the great fortresses at York and Chester.

198 SEVERUS sends VIRIUS LUPUS to Britain to repair the havoc wrought by the Barbarians. LUPUS, and after him ALFENUS SENECIO, reconstructs Hadrian's Wall between 198–208.

208 SEVERUS in person attacks the Caledonians. He penetrates nearly to the extreme northern tip of Britain.

211 Worn out by his arduous campaign in Scotland, SEVERUS dies at York. But his work of pacification in Britain is effective. Britain enjoys peace during the subsequent upheavals elsewhere in the Empire.

286 The Admiral of the British fleet, M. AURELIUS CARAU-SIUS, sets up Britain as an independent empire. The two Augusti, DIOCLETIAN and MAXIMIAN, acknowledge the picturesque CARAUSIUS as one of themselves. In addition to Britain, he is allotted a strip of N. France.

293 DIOCLETIAN's general, CONSTANTIUS CHLORUS, is instructed to seize CARAUSIUS' French possessions. Meanwhile CARAUSIUS is murdered by the contemptible ALLECTUS, his finance minister.

296 CONSTANTIUS crosses the Channel and defeats ALLEC-TUS, who is slain in battle. CONSTANTIUS, vigorous and popular, effects widespread reorganization in Britain.

306 CONSTANTIUS, after a protracted encounter with the Picts, dies at York. His son, known to history as CON-STANTINE THE GREAT, assumes the title of CAESAR IMPERATOR.

337 CONSTANS, son of CONSTANTINE, fights the Picts (from Scotland) and the Scots (from Ireland).

350 CONSTANS is murdered, MAGNUS MAGNENTIUS, the Gaulish usurper, is killed by CONSTANTIUS II, together with the beloved MATINUS, *vicarius* of Britain.

360 The cruel LUPICINUS is sent to Britain.

368 In the reign of VALENTINIAN I, a concerted attack is made on Britain, by Picts, Scots, Saxons, Franks, and Attacotti (a confederation of tribes in Ireland). The Roman troops are everywhere routed. VALENTINIAN despatches the Spanish COUNT THEODOSIUS to clear the country of the barbarians, installed throughout the entire land. THEODOSIUS carries out the difficult mission successfully.

383 MAGNUS MAXIMUS denudes Britain of its garrison to seize the throne of the Empire from VALENTINIAN's son GRATIAN, who is murdered. Britain, left defenceless, once more succumbs to barbarian hordes. Hadrian's Wall makes its last defence.

393 STILICHO, regent in Britain of the Emperor THEO-DOSIUS, son of COUNT THEODOSIUS, once again liberates Britain.

399 STILICHO completes the war of liberation. He enlists the aid of CUNEDDA, a British chieftain, to help in the work of pacification.

401 STILICHO is forced to withdraw troops from Britain to

help protect the Empire from the advancing Goths.

403 ALARIC the Goth is defeated at Verona. RADAGAISUS begins a fresh Gothic invasion.

405 The troops in Britain, in despair, set up successive usurpers called MARCUS, GRATIAN, and finally CONSTAN-TINE to provide for the defence of the country.

410 The Emperor HONORIUS tells the people of Britain that Rome is no longer in a position to come to their aid. STILICHO has been murdered, and ALARIC is marching on Rome. HONORIUS' rescript marks the end of the Roman occupation of Britain, though at the time both Rome and Britain believed that their fortunes would sooner or later be reunited.

430 By this date the government of Britain is being decisively taken over by the Saxons.

446 The British make a last appeal to AETIUS. The appeal is rejected. The bond with Rome is completely sundered.

ANGLO-SAXON, VIKING, AND NORMAN TIMES

AD

313 Roman toleration of Christianity.

410 Roman protection withdrawn.

410–c. 520 Settlement of England by Saxons.

c. 432 St. Patrick goes to Ireland.

467–93 The legend of Arthur may rest on a British king who resisted the Saxon invaders at this time.

519 CERDIC and CYNRIC (kings of West Saxons).

520 Britons win battle at Mount Bedon.

545–6 *De Excidio*—Gildas.

547 IDA, King of Bernicia.

552 West Saxons take Old Sarum (near Salisbury).

560 ÆTHELBERT, King of Kent, d. 616.

c. 563 St. Columba goes to Iona.

568 Æthelbert defeated by West Saxons.

c. 570 Birth of Mohammed at Mecca.

571 West Saxons invade Mid-Britain.

577 West Saxons win battle at Deorham.

584 West Saxons defeated at Faddiley.

588 ÆTHELRIC, King of Northumbria.

593 ÆTHELRITH, King of Northumbria, *d.* 617.

597 Landing of Augustine. He restores St. Martin's Church at Canterbury.

603 Battle of Daegsasten.

613 Battle of Chester.

617 EADWINE, King of Northumbria, *d.* 633.

625 Conversion of Eadwine. Paulinus converts Northumbria.

626 PENDA, King of Mercians, *d.* 655.

626 Supremacy of Eadwine.

633 OSWALD, King of Bernicia, *d.* 641.

633 Eadwine killed at Hatfield by Mercians.

633 Defeat of Welsh by Oswald.

635 Aidan goes to Holy Island.

c. 640 Conversion of Wessex.

650–60 Sutton Hoo Ship Burial.

654 OSWIN, King of Northumbria. *d.* 670.

655 Battle at Winwaed.

658 West Saxons invade to the Parret.

659 WULFHERE, King of Mercia.

661 West Saxons retreat across the Thames.

664 Council of Whitby. Caedmon at Whitby.

668 Theodore of Tarsus, Archbishop of Canterbury.

670 ECGFRITH, King of Northumbria, *d.* 685.

670–80 Brixworth Church, Northants. Wing Church, Bucks. St. Pancras Church, Canterbury. Bewcastle and Ruthwell Crosses.

673 Birth of Bede.

675 ÆTHELRED, King of Mercia, *d.* 704.

681 Completion of English conversion. South Saxons embrace Christianity under Wilfrid; heathen burials cease.

681 Crypt at Hexham built.

681 The Lindisfarne Gospels.

682 Escomb Church, Durham.

687 Death of St. Cuthbert.

688 INE, King of West Saxons, *d.* 726.

688 Conquest of Mid-Somerset by Wessex.

c. 700 Franks Casket (Northumbria).

715 Bradford-on-Avon Church.

716 ÆTHELBALD, King of Mercia, *d.* 757.

716 Defeat of Mercia by West Saxons.

c. 730 Bede, the first English historian, writes his Ecclesiastical History.
733 Mercia conquers Wessex.
735 Death of Bede.
753 Death of Boniface.
754 Wessex wins Battle of Burford.
757 OFFA, King of Mercia, *d.* 796.
775 Mercia subdues Kent.
792 Sack of Lindisfarne by the Vikings.
793 Foundation of St. Albans Monastery.
796 COENWULF, King of Mercia, *d.* 821.
c. 800 Historia Brittorium (Nennius).
802 ECGBERHT, King of Wessex, *d.* 839.
815 Final conquest of British.
828 Supremacy of Ecgberht.
837 Defeat of Danes by Ecgberht.
839 ÆTHELWULF, King of Wessex, *d.* 858.
849 Birth of Ælfred.
851 Defeat of Danes at Aclca.
857 ÆTHELBALD, King of Wessex, *d.* 860.
860 ÆTHELBERT, King of Wessex, *d.* 866.
066 Danes land in East Anglia.
867 Danes conquer Northumbria and capture York.
867 St. Michael's Church, St. Albans.
c. 868 Martyrdom of Eadmund.
871 ÆLFRED, King of Wessex, *d.* 899.
871 Danes invade East Anglia and Wessex.
878 Ælfred wins battle at Edington—Peace of Wedmore.
891–2 Start of compilation of Anglo-Saxon Chronicle.
897 Ælfred builds a Fleet.
899 EADWARD THE ELDER, *d.* 925.
912 Northmen attack Normandy.
912 Deerhurst Church, Glos.
925 ÆTHELSTAN, *d.* 939.
939 EADMUND, *d.* 946.
943 Dunstan, Abbot of Glastonbury.
946 EADRED, *d.* 955.
954 Submission of Danelaw—England becomes one kingdom.
955 EADWIG, *d.* 959.
958 EADGAR, *d.* 975.

959   Dunstan, Archbishop of Canterbury.
975   EADWARD THE MARTYR, *d.* 979.
978   ÆTHELRED THE UNREADY, *d. 1016.*
978   Benedictine rule introduced.
978   Worth Church, Sussex.
991   Vikings defeat East Anglians at Maldon.
991   Barnack Church, Northants.
1013   England submits to Swein.
1016   EADMUND IRONSIDE, *d.* 1016.
1016   CNUT, *d.* 1035.
1016   Breamore Church, Hants.
1027   Birth of William of Normandy.
1037   HARALD, *d.* 1040.
1037   Earls Barton Church, Northants.
1042   EADWARD THE CONFESSOR, *d.* 1066.
1051   Bosham Church, Sussex.
1054–6   Normans conquer Southern Italy.
1060   Normans invade Sicily.
1060–80   Close of paganism in Scandinavia.
1066   HAROLD.
1066   Harold defeats Hardrada at Stamford Bridge and is
          defeated himself at Senlac.
1066   WILLIAM THE CONQUEROR.
1070   Lanfranc, Archbishop of Canterbury, reorganizes
          Church.
c. 1080   St. Benet Church, Cambridge. Sompting Church,
          Sussex.
1086   Domesday Book completed.

INDEX

The numerals in bold type refer to the figure numbers of the illustrations